THE ART OF THE GREAT HOLLYWOOD
PORTRAIT PHOTOGRAPHERS
1925-1940

THE ART OF THE GREAT HOLLYWOOD PORTRAIT PHOTOGRAPHERS 1925-1940

by John Kobal

Harrison House
New York

This 1987 edition is published by Harrison House, distributed by
Crown Publishers, Inc., 225 Park Avenue South, New York,
New York 10003, by arrangement with John Kobal.
Printed and bound in Italy

Library of Congress Cataloging-in-Publication Data

Kobal, John.
   The art of the great Hollywood portrait photographers,
1925–1940.

   Originally published: 1st ed. New York : Knopf :
Distributed by Random House, 1980.
   Bibliography: p.
   Includes index.
   1. Glamour photography.   2. Photography—Portraits.
3. Photography—California—Hollywood.   I. Title.
TR678.K6   1987   /79'.2'0973   87-15035
ISBN 0-517-64102-X
              h g f e d c b a

To Victoria Wilson, the editor one dreams of,
who got me into it and helped me out of it

Contents

Acknowledgments

Very special thanks go to Paul Morrissey for pointing me in the direction, and to Ross Woodman, Erika Cheetham, and John Russell Taylor for, each in his or her own way, illuminating an important part of my journey. Many others have helped me with knowledge shared and time offered, making this work a great joy for me. Hilary Downey and Roselyne Gregor typed and retyped not only with endless good patience but with an enthusiasm and interest that refired my own excitement; Marc Gervais, Loretta Young, Juliet Colman Toland, Katharine Hepburn, Louise Brooks, Tom Jones, Mrs. Cecilia De Mille Harper, Florence Cole, and Henry Thoresby gave generously of their knowledge and encouraged me in various stages of the manuscript; and the great photographers George Hurrell, Clarence S. Bull, Laszlo Willinger, and Ted Allan made prints especially for this book from their own original negatives.

I am deeply indebted to the men and women—photographers, publicists, and stars—whose memories I tapped, whose photographs I borrowed, and whose patience with my ignorance was noble. This book is also dedicated to them.

THE ART OF THE GREAT HOLLYWOOD
PORTRAIT PHOTOGRAPHERS

1925-1940

No woman in art or literature was more lovingly created than the visionary maid born of Josef von Sternberg's longing to work with Greta Garbo and ultimately revealed in the splendid creature whom we recognize as Marlene Dietrich aboard the *Shanghai Express*.

In the movie, von Sternberg uses the dialogue between Clive Brook, the Karenin-like hero, and Dietrich—two former lovers reunited accidentally—to establish an image of one type of woman: fatal and decadent. She is a creature seemingly without a heart who scorns the conventional role of the fallen woman. Early in the film, Dietrich stands looking from the window of the train before it has pulled out of the station in Shanghai. The corridor on either side and the compartments behind her are swarming with passengers. Dietrich turns and sees Brook leaning out of the adjoining window. The clamor and activity give them privacy. It has been a five-year separation. She replies to his question of "Married?" with a bemused smile that seems to mock his self-detached air. "No," she says, adding, slowly and coolly, the syllables divided by pauses, "It took more than one man to change my name to Shanghai Lily," the notorious white flower of China. And as their conversation takes place, Sternberg, in a succession of haunting close-ups of Dietrich, creates his luminous vision of love, endless and true.

Dietrich has attributed all she ever was and ever would be to von Sternberg—a compliment he himself rejected. Few stars understood the importance of the camera better than Dietrich.

According to the people who worked with them, nothing was too much for Dietrich to endure if it achieved the effect the director was after. For one scene in *The Scarlet Empress* (1934), she ran down an elaborate staircase forty-five times in her cumbersome eighteenth-century costume before von Sternberg approved the wordless scene. John

Engstead, who years later became the official photographer for her celebrated one-woman show, recalled that for her last film with von Sternberg, Paramount's *The Devil Is a Woman* (1935), the designer Travis Banton and Dietrich produced an enormous Spanish comb which supported a large mantilla. The comb was anchored to Dietrich's head with wires wound into the little braids of her hair. Her agony was apparent only when, at the end of each day, her hairdresser released the comb with wire cutters, and "Marlene fell forward, arms and head resting on her dressing table, exhausted from pain. When she came up, tears were running down her face."

Marlene Dietrich, 1930. Photographed by Eugene R. Richee for Paramount. Dietrich had not yet made an American film and had only been at Paramount for a few weeks. In this, from one of the first official sessions, the studio wanted to project her as a new Garbo. Dietrich's German look remains, but the glamourization has begun; Josef von Sternberg's lighting gives her the delicate cheekbones and large eyes.

Though she played a passive role in von Sternberg's creation, Dietrich understood and actively pursued the part, recognizing that this collaboration not only enabled him to do his best work but produced results of which she herself could be proud. Ironically, it was her conscious pursuit of his genius that turned Dietrich into von Sternberg's very own, near-fatal *"belle dame."*

The results of her portrait sessions, during her time with von Sternberg and after it, justify the pride expressed when she told Banton that her studio photographs were of greater importance to her than her films. Dietrich applied the same dedication and hard work she brought to her films to the obligatory sittings in the studio portrait gallery, which had developed from makeshift camera sets into an elaborately staffed and appointed workshop.

For the sake of an interesting photograph, Dietrich thought nothing of leaning over a chair, unsupported in a backbreaking position, for minutes on end while von Sternberg explored her face with lights—a high spot to bring out the shadows under her cheekbones, another to shade very slightly the top of her forehead in order to round out her face. To achieve the dreamlike quality he was after, von Sternberg ordered that a piece of very sheer *mousseline de soie* in a little cardboard ring be placed in front of the lens. This technique was adopted by many other photographers; but without von Sternberg's vision and Dietrich's force, the hallucinatory quality seemed sentimental, while in the hands of inferior photographers, it became a mere screen to obscure wrinkles for those stars who lacked Dietrich's natural radiance.

When everything was at last as he wished, von Sternberg would stand behind the photographer and direct both of them: Dietrich's lids would lower, her mouth would part, and mystery would fill her face. Those early photographs, with their tones of purest white and black and all the shades of gray in between, were taken at the height of Dietrich's fame (1930–1935) by Eugene R. Richee, Don English, and William Walling, Jr. The results of this creative union—built on time shared and a striving to divine an original look—produced a school dedicated to and for beauty, radically different from our contemporary aesthetic of "sincerity" and pseudorealism.

To appreciate their power in a photographic context, one has to look not at other portraits but at the landscapes of Walker Evans; at the social-conscious documentary images sponsored by Roosevelt's Farm Security Administration; at the still lifes and females nudes of Edward Weston; at surrealistic street scenes of glistening-wet pavements and chrome-plated cars with jeweled occupants that are a blur of speeding light.

(Above) Marlene Dietrich, 1931. Photographed by Eugene R. Richee. One year, one film (Morocco), and several hundred portraits later, Dietrich and von Sternberg are moving steadily closer to the creation of that extraordinary creature who was more a work of art than an evocation of Dietrich's personality (see the portrait by Willinger, page 275). Her cheekbones are great wide plains, and her eyebrows have been redesigned to create a larger space between eye and brow for von Sternberg's lights to play across and build on. Note her hands trailing off into the shadows. Though her fingers are actually short and stubby, they are posed to give the illusion of being long and sinuous.

(Right) Marlene Dietrich, 1932. Photographed by Don English on the set of Shanghai Express. To von Sternberg the essential contribution of film to dramatic expression was the close-up of the human face: the camera moving beyond the merely physical, beyond the face, through the eyes, into the emotions of the character. In Shanghai Express, Dietrich's third American film with von Sternberg, and in this photograph, his vision and their collaboration were realized.

When I mounted an exhibition entitled Hollywood Portrait Photography, 1927–1941, at the Victoria and Albert Museum in London in 1974 (the first exhibition devoted to the Hollywood group), the portraits should have been interspersed with photographs of the urban poor taken during the Depression—not to make the obvious point-counterpoint but to round out a view of society that is incomplete without them.

Those who choose to see the great Hollywood stars simply in terms of the conditions out of which they emerged—economic, political, social, or technological—stop short of what was actually produced: of what emerged out of their existence. These portraits of the great faces of Hollywood were products of their time and were forged by a need so powerful that these images were able to transcend both their time and the need they fulfilled—something that conventional portraits, chained to their subjects and our knowledge of them, can never be. They possess a freshness and openness to be found only in children, and an intensity most common in the mad. Long after the individual reputations of the subjects of these portraits have been forgotten, their profound beauty will cause them to live on—as have Raphael's Madonnas and Botticelli's angels; Gainsborough's society beauties and Romney's portraits of Emma Hamilton. These are also works by artists who succeeded in conveying something more than just a sitter whose beauty held an age enthralled. By creating a romantic ideal, as did the Hollywood photographers represented here, these painters showed beauty to have been the source of their inspiration.

Their success was variable: not every painter is a Leonardo, nor every star a Garbo. But surely it is no accident that two of the best-known works of art are such glorifications of beauty—the sensual Venus de Milo, by an unknown Greek sculptor of the second century B.C., and Leonardo da Vinci's Mona Lisa. It is a tribute to Leonardo's achievement that many art critics and biographers still question the gender of his sitter; although idealized, its sexuality is indisputable. Though Josef von Sternberg's "Dietrich in drag" as an aspect of the 1930's was one of our aesthetic ideals, the Venus found on Melos, firmly double chinned and ample thighed, remains—even armless—as whole in form and as sexual. George Hurrell's elegant studies of Norma Shearer are every bit as ravishing and erotic as Fragonard's gently sweeping creatures. Shearer's beauty, like that of Madame de Pompadour, may have depended more on dazzle and expression than on bone structure, but her photographers served her better than did Pompadour's painters (of the many paintings done of Pompadour, her brother is supposed to have said that none looked alike and none looked like her). What Shearer's eyes lacked in size they made up in

Marlene Dietrich, 1934, The Devil Is a Woman, *directed by Josef von Sternberg (Paramount). Photographed by William Walling, Jr.*

8

brightness, wittiness, and a sparkle that make them seem to be what they should have been, had Nature been kinder.

If the written history of these stars were to be lost, so that future historians and students of art might find it necessary to debate the genders of some of the faces gazing from these pages (note the intense, almost masculine energy emanating from Crawford, the ambivalence in Garbo, the passive splendor of the young Gary Cooper), these photographs by the great Hollywood portrait photographers would not be diminished. Each image reveals a coming together of the flesh and the spirit to create an ideal to which others aspired.

If male images in art haven't quite the hold on our imaginations (with a few remarkable exceptions, such as Michelangelo's David and the celebrated Discobolus, a bronze statue of heroic size in violent action by the Greek sculptor Myron of the fifth century B.C.) as do female images, it is not because of a lack of attention to men by artists. One thinks of the many statues by Greek sculptors, notably Praxiteles, whose lifelike works in marble were celebrated in songs and poems by the praise singers of their day. Many of those graceful, sinuously posed antique gods and athletes were the inspiration for male physique photography and for many of the best-remembered studies of early film matinee idols, such as Francis X. Bushman, Rudolph Valentino, and Douglas Fairbanks, Sr.

The most interesting works of art from any period do more than just record the general image of their era; they help create and illuminate that image. Our picture of the Renaissance draws greatly on da Vinci, and of the baroque period on Rubens; eighteenth-century Europe had the landscape of a Canaletto, but its face was that of Gainsborough's society and Watteau's *fêtes galantes*. The decline of the Austrian Empire was briefly checked in Winterhalter's glamorous paintings, filled with the dreamy Straussian empress and her court; while the American John Singer Sargent was probably the last portrait painter to capture his age—as, for instance, in his elegant portrait of a satin-skinned woman in a low-cut black velvet gown and long black gloves. *Madame X** (1884) provoked a scandal and inspired the famous French boulevard melodrama of the same name about a society lady who sinned and paid—and paid and paid. . . . Erotic and revealing without the benefit of a romanticized backdrop, Sargent's startling departure from conventional portrait style made his sitter ask that her name be removed when the portrait was exhibited.

---

* The look and erotic current underlying Rita Hayworth's teasing dance number "Put the Blame on Mame" in *Gilda* (1946), choreographed by Jack Cole, were inspired by this Sargent painting.

Norma Shearer, 1932, Smilin' Through (MGM). Photographed by George Hurrell. Costume by Adrian.

Joan Crawford, 1935, No More Ladies *(MGM). Photographed by George Hurrell.*

Gary Cooper, 1928, Beau Sabreur *(Paramount). Photographed by Eugene R. Richee.*

It had been earlier in that century that poets had turned to the celebration of human beauty as inspiration for their art. But even as artists more or less ceased to concern themselves directly with the representation of human beauty, poets foreshadowed visions that the camera was to capture, while offering a definition of the future achievements of Hollywood photographers. Sir Walter Scott, searching for a term that would spell magic and enchantment, had introduced into the literary language an old Scottish word that defined those striking, alluring images of nearly a hundred years later: *glamour* conveyed a magical or fictitious beauty attached to a person and has always been used to describe Hollywood romanticism.

The inspirational source from which the poets drew—and out of

Robert Taylor, 1936. Photographed by George Hurrell (MGM).

Greta Garbo, 1929, The Kiss *(MGM). Photographed by Clarence S. Bull.*

which came the vision of Moneta in Keats's "Hyperion," the veiled maid in Shelley's "Alastor," and the "Phantom of delight" that was Wordsworth's "perfect Woman"—was to have its cinematic equivalent in the camera's lens, through which faces moved as if in a wondrous dream. Coleridge wrote (in his *Biographia Literaria*): "Grant me a nature having two contrary forces, the one which tends to expand indefinitely, while the other strives to apprehend or find itself in this infinity, and I will cause the world of intelligences with the whole system of representatives to rise up before you."

These portraits by studio photographers are the result of a rare collaboration: the same artist and subject working together to produce the third thing, with the artist given total access to his extraordinary models, and all of the money and time necessary—ranging from days to a decade. They were to create a style that could instantly identify a product for which there was no precedent, not even in photography. The task was not merely to photograph established celebrities, of which the movies had introduced a rich source, but to help create something entirely new, something that had never existed before—a breed of celebrity with the extraordinary power to transfix. These photographs were born out of the union between the "gods and goddesses" of the Hollywood of the thirties and the artists who were able to apprehend that quality in an image. We saw it. And worshiped it.

It is not altogether surprising that the style of the studio photographers should emerge with the Depression and flourish dramatically during the bleakest years before settling into a mold of conventional glamour.

Up to the mid-1920's, American movies had grown with their audience, reflecting their progress, carefree optimism, and easy successes. Once unemployment swept the country, Hollywood movies, to hold on to their public, could not afford to mirror their despair in realistic terms. Now the star system, which had existed since 1911, assumed a truly exalted role, fulfilling a sudden and dramatic need in people's lives. The quality that had made stars unique would now make Hollywood itself unique. American movies had always manufactured entertainment— more successful, perhaps, but otherwise not much different from popular novels or sports, vaudeville, comic books, records, or radio—but not since their beginnings, and never again, had they achieved so meaningful a purpose: to provide hope through identification. The product had not become more socially significant, but the man in the street took his lead from the hero on the screen. For years the audience had mindlessly fol-

Rudolph Valentino, 1921, The Sheik (Paramount). Photographed by Donald Biddle Keyes. Paramount was the first studio to have its own portrait gallery. The impetus came from Keyes, who headed the gallery until he left to become a cameraman. This was one of the first photographs taken there.

(Left) Joel McCrea, 1932, Bird of Paradise (RKO). *Photographed by Ernest Bachrach. At the time of this photograph, RKO was grooming McCrea, who had been with them for about a year, to become their Gary Cooper/Clark Gable. "If the player is a newcomer to the studio," Bachrach said, "I must make my camera see his or her personality as the public will discover it on the screen many months hence."*

(Right) Douglas Fairbanks, Jr., 1930. *Photographed by Elmer Fryer (Warner Bros.).*

lowed the adventures and copied the look; now they copied the attitude— Gable, Crawford, Dietrich, Cooper, Stanwyck, Colbert, Lombard, Cagney, Davis. . . . It wasn't the plane that crossed the Atlantic that captured people's imaginations, but the man who flew it. It wasn't the escapist stories Hollywood churned out that gained our adoration, but the people who cut through them. The stars were not the fantasies they were subsequently made out to be, but their great faces, casting their glamour from gigantic billboards across the nation, burned as beacons, capable of guiding people to the spirit within themselves.

The Hollywood studio still photographers moved away from the pale

20

portraits of the twenties and created pictures that bore witness to the spirit and imagination in everyone, despite the exigencies of everyday life. If we could not always realize our own individuality, we could and did recognize and admire that of others. Ray Jones (see Notes on Other Photographers), who headed the portrait gallery at Universal from 1935 to the 1950's, believed that behind the public's insatiable desire to identify with its favorite actor or actress was the fact that "in the mind of every beholder there is an ideal of beauty that can never be found. . . . Perhaps on the screen we could discover the elusive qualities that have brought these actors fame and fortune."

Feathers flare from Marlene Dietrich's perfumed shoulder pads like natural appendages that would enable her to fly off at a moment's notice, like any other bird of paradise; there is Joan Crawford, again and again, her passion for posing as compelling as it is apparent, the concentration of profoundly felt suffering in a few finely sculpted contours on her forehead.

These images belong to an experience. The finest among them create an emotional empathy akin to that found in a bar of music, a line of poetry, or a canvas filled with color. There are portraits of Jean Harlow, tantalizing, transfigured, emerging, gazing outward from a radium pool of light—atomic energy streaming from her hair and from the pores of her skin—her beauty emphasized like gangbusters. The awkward traces of her heavy-boned face and body, the unclassic cleft in her chin, the too-small, sunken eyes—all have been modulated, enlarged, or retouched to harmonize into a glorious whole. It leaves us with an impression that encapsulates the film in which she starred and for whose promotion the photograph was taken. In this instance, *Reckless* (MGM, 1935), a pedestrian five-and-ten-cent tale, she is a musical star who marries Mr. High Society and is wrongly blamed when her dissolute husband kills himself. Left with their child to raise and her in-laws to fight, she turns to the stage hoping to make a comeback and a living (this was loosely based on the drama surrounding blues singer Libby Holman, whose millionaire husband was shot under mysterious circumstances). Harlow's climactic appearance on the stage is greeted by a hostile silence. She begins to sing. After a few bars, a barrage of jeers and catcalls make it impossible for her to go on. She confronts the audience. Her face in close-up silences the mob in a long shot. With defiantly squared shoulders set off luxuriantly in silver lamé, she demands to be heard and judged for her art and not for their opinions of her as a woman. An audacious scene,

John Wayne, 1931. Photographed by William A. Fraker for Columbia.

this, as much for the actress on the stage as for the star on the screen, since the public of that time, flocking to see the new Harlow picture, was likely to recall at this point the facts of Harlow's private life of a few years earlier. She leans imperiously against the high-vaulted proscenium arch, and in a voice that couldn't carry beyond the first row of any theatre, but shot in a tight close-up to reach out and hold every last row in every cinema balcony in the world, she sings her song of redemption.

It is here that the miracle occurred, and this glistening, shimmering, lavishly mounted piece of art-decorated nonsense justified itself. This was the reason for the movie; this was why hundreds of men and women had spent thousands of hours laboring. This was the reason Jean Harlow was a star while all the other platinum blondes were chorus girls. It was the sacrificial moment—this huge close-up of Harlow, refracting the intense battery of the studio's enormous arc lights as they concentrated on her face, her hair, her neck and alabaster shoulders—a living conflagration of energy. This moment, with all that led up to it, is there in the portraits taken of her by the studio's photographers. Long after the details of the image have been forgotten, the impact will remain.

The industry that required this product employed thousands of men and women whose full-time function it was to find people of rare physical beauty—like Hedy Lamarr, a star to whom the astute David O. Selznick once referred in a memo as having "actually been established purely by photography"—or, even more important, to find individuals with the potential of altering their looks to create a compelling visual ideal that would stand as a statement of our desires and our need for fulfillment—a Jean Harlow, a Norma Shearer, a Clark Gable, or a Gloria Swanson. The quest was for that face which would provoke in millions of others the desire to identify: for if the movie-goer desires, then he must be desired; if he fears, then he must be feared; if he loves, then he must be loved. The great stars had this deeply motivated skill for distorting and modifying themselves which complemented the photographers' skill of creating from those faces extraordinary creatures.

In close-up on the big screen, the star transcended himself or herself by creating another whole image and was living proof of the ancient and honorable urge extolled by the poets. Movie stars were worshiped as the triumph of the hope and faith that people have revealed for a second or two in the bathroom mirror or caught in the look of a lover. One is tempted to see an analogy in the story of Lady Hamilton. Did her worldly lover fall in love with Emma Lyon, the blacksmith's daughter, or was it rather with the brilliantly colored beauty created by the painter Romney, whose portraits idealized her? Did Aly Khan fall in love with Margarita

Marion Davies, 1919. Photographed by Arnold Genthe in New York. By this time Davies had left the Ziegfeld Follies to star in motion pictures. The face in the photograph is romanticized, though saved from the saccharine by Genthe's delicate lighting. It is Marion Davies as the Victorians might have seen her, rather than the contemporary beauty the Hollywood photographers were able to achieve.

Carmen Cansino, the daughter of a Spanish dancer, or with the ideal of beauty known as Rita Hayworth?

The physical appearances that are presented in these photographs were images of a type that had never existed before, either in painting or photography. The influence of the portraits of an earlier great photographer like Baron Adolf de Meyer are easily traceable to painters such as Whistler, Boldini, and Sargent. Up until the late twenties, portrait photography followed the traditional format of painting, presenting the figure either

Joan Crawford, 1932, Letty Lynton (MGM). Photographed by George Hurrell.

Jean Harlow, 1935, Reckless (MGM). Photographed by George Hurrell. "I kept the shadows strong on the face whether they were heavy or minor shadows, so that they designed the face instead of making it flat."

full-length or from the waist up, usually accompanied and described by the paraphernalia of the period. The early star portraits were much like those found in photographic studios in any fair-sized American town. Later, though, the publicity and advertising branches of the film industry required widespread recognition of their artists' faces, preferably from magazine covers first seen at a distance and able to survive even the cheapest printing processes. The close-up image of the face was established as the standard format of the Hollywood photographic portrait, and the powers of the close-up were brought from the screen to the still.

From this period came the definitive image of beauty for the twentieth century—the face of Greta Garbo. Since her emergence in the late twenties as the finest dramatic star of the silent era, her portraits by Ruth

(Left) Mae Murray, 1918. Photographed by Baron Adolf de Meyer.

(Right) Greta Garbo, 1929, The Kiss *(MGM). Photographed by Clarence S. Bull.*

MG-5277

Harriet Louise, who headed her own portrait gallery at Metro-Goldwyn-Mayer from 1925 to 1930, and by Clarence Sinclair Bull, from 1930 to 1942, became the standard of beauty in our time.

The only later photographs that approximated these are George Hurrell's extraordinary dramatic portraits of Joan Crawford, which present her as possessed of an intense love of life, and various photographers' portraits of Marlene Dietrich, all of them subject to a lighting arrangement and style created for her by von Sternberg.

From the thousands of still images taken of the great stars of the twenties and thirties, two recognizable types emerge: the inward-gazing and the outward-looking. The inward-gazing were the true immortals, the Buddhas among the stars, wrapped in a world of their own, approached only through the gradual cessation of desire. They offered an invitation to transcend; the price of admission: death. There was Garbo, of course; Valentino; Louise Brooks, whose celebrated beauty incarnated Wedekind's force of nature, the fatal Lulu she became for the Pabst films; and Dietrich in von Sternberg's films, though not in the foolish ones she made after splitting with him, which tried to retain his highly personal conception of her but without the formal context required for its existence, with the inevitable result that she ended up looking more forlorn than remote, drifting aimlessly in and out of desert sands and Russian swamps, from setup to sunset, her voice occasionally floating by an overhead mike, calling plaintively, "Joe, Joe. . . ." But Dietrich is a survivor. So it was not at all surprising that this remarkable woman would discard the persona they had created together to reveal her own, with which she scored a triumph in *Destry Rides Again* (Universal, 1939) and continued as one of the outward-looking archetypes.

The outward-looking were the mediators between the remote immortals and ourselves, beckoning and inviting, offering themselves in a variety of ways, each one defining a style, though none granting final satisfaction. They moved between the two worlds, larger and more generous than life, but not quite so large as death. The young Cary Grant, emerging from second leads to stardom, is caught, in a portrait by Robert Coburn (see page 31), at that moment of transition: feminine softness subtly shifting into a masculine polo-sweatered sexiness; ambition exuded with disarming candor from the too-knowing eyes of this bronzed fantasy lover. Another whose look belies her passive poses is the young Carole Lombard, emulating the Dietrich languor with lids half-closed but eyes, one feels, wide open with laughter, should anyone take her too seriously.

Joan Crawford, 1930. Photographed by George Hurrell. As a young painter, Hurrell supplemented his income by taking pictures of his fellow artists and their patrons, some of whom found his photographs more compelling than his canvases. "I had an attitude about lighting that was different," he said, "even about the lens quality. All the other photographers were using a Vertone lens, which created a diffusion. I shot sharp, extremely sharp. That immediately gave the photograph character." From the moment he arrived at MGM in 1929, a few months before he took this photograph of Crawford, Hurrell knew what such a portrait should be. The concept of glamour came into its own in his pictures, and he achieved this by photographing the great faces of Hollywood—among them Shearer, Gable, and Harlow—without makeup. No one before him had dared to do this. Afterward it became standard practice.

Later still there is Rita Hayworth, whose successful portraits are those that capture the dynamism of her movement and hold it in a perfectly balanced moment of stillness.*

Inward or outward, we respond instinctively to these archetypes; they are larger than life. Those stars who waver between these two well-defined images risk the fall from grace, and those who disappoint our expecta-

Louise Brooks, 1929.
Photographed by James Abbe.

Cary Grant, 1935.
Photographed by Robert Coburn.

* Robert Coburn, Hayworth's photographer at Columbia for more than fifteen years, spoke in an interview of her growing frustration at his efforts to manipulate her mood toward the quintessential Hayworth over-the-shoulder "come hither" look, which the front office demanded to help sell her films.

tions are rarely given a second chance. The most striking exception is Katharine Hepburn.

From the outset she held herself apart, intriguing us even while she resisted definition. Interested in neither subservience nor possession, she provided an inspiration to self-discipline—though this quality, evident in the portraits taken in the first phase of her film career (at RKO in the thirties), didn't emerge on the screen until twenty years later. Hepburn, like Bette Davis and Barbara Stanwyck, was no conventional "glamour puss"; but unlike those two superb women, she was what the French call *une belle laide.* It made her a natural for the camera.

From the beginning, Hepburn's Hollywood portraits by Ernest Bachrach hinted at the reality that lay beneath her intimidating screen image, in which class and breeding were disdainfully tossed out at the audience to make them feel like a poor Stella Dallas at her daughter's wedding. By the end of the decade, the public had almost ceased to care about her.

In her portrayal of the socially superior Tracy Lord in *The Philadelphia Story* (1940), which the playwright Philip Barry had written for her, we at last begin to see on film the Hepburn we had been drawn to in the portraits. Here the still feverishly overactive spoiled brat is brought down to earth. She is told by a man of the people (James Stewart) that she is not a creature of ice but a real woman, wondrously alive and made for love. At this moment, her transformation occurs. Stewart woos her on our behalf. Hepburn, dressed by Adrian, incandescently lit and photographed by Joseph Ruttenberg, looking more beautiful in close-up than she had ever been on film before, sways, trembles, succumbs, and—with Stewart as our envoy—wins us. Her film career began in earnest.

In Hepburn's next film, *Woman of the Year* (1942), the first to team her with Spencer Tracy, his strength and his appreciation of her, clear from their first moment on the screen together, set her free from her crippling mannerisms. She no longer needed to race to keep her place. We the audience could now relax and enjoy her, as the perfect partners sparred in words, looks, and actions throughout their films, their individuality never sacrificed, their mutual growth assured.

These images, viewed as a group, evoke a kind of power, mystery, and soulfulness that seems to have vanished in photography almost as suddenly as it appeared. By the end of the thirties the spirit behind them had begun to wane. The photographs of the forties lack excitement; they are sprayed with advertising-poster colors—pillar-box-red lips, blue-horizon eyes—

Carole Lombard, 1932. Photographed by Eugene R. Richee. The influence of von Sternberg is evident in the overhead lighting that sculpts Lombard's forehead and shoulders and reveals the shape of her legs.

34

turning something that had been intensely powerful into something that was too bright, too cheery, and ultimately empty. If the public raised no objection, it was because their minds were elsewhere—soldiers, generals, and presidents were their heroes; stars were now a candy-coated version of the boy and girl next door. The forties' star, brightly lit and colored, was the ultimate Disney cartoon.

By 1942 Hurrell had left Hollywood; many of his colleagues were in the service. The young men who had trained as their assistants and who now replaced them at the studios photographed the forties stars to conform to the established notion of glamour, but their portraits no longer had that rush of excitement or the sense of discovery that was so apparent in the studio portraits of the thirties.

This was partly the photographers' fault. They were either too young to demand their rights or had grown older and settled, their jobs secured by stringent union contracts and their spirits worn by years of fighting with publicity department heads who preferred formula to form, quantity to content, speed to style. It was easier to give in. In addition, the Second World War had given the film industry a captive audience, and, typically short-sighted, Hollywood failed to look within itself for solutions or ideas. Instead, it submitted to the demands of the new photo journals, like *Life* and *Look,* which prided themselves on capturing the so-called human quality of the star. (While these publications credited their own "candid-snapshot" photographers, they rarely gave individual photographers credit when they used the precise, carefully posed studio stills.) These factors coincided with the rise of a public for whom stars were again what they had been before the Depression. Though movie stars still figured in the public's dreams, they were no longer a profound part of everyday life.

By the 1950's even that had gone. The business had degenerated into the creation of artifacts that lacked redeeming virtue, and without energy to revitalize and excite, banality and boredom could not be disguised. What was offensive about these images, as well as the films, was their mindlessness. They offered neither inspiration nor escape.

Only in the world of fashion does there still exist a venue for art in photographing beauty that suggests the elusive qualities that came so readily in the Hollywood photographs of forty-five and fifty years ago.

In the photographic portrait the selection of the carefully arranged form and content was securely within the control of the photographer. An awareness of who or what the subject was thus becomes essential to our appreciation of such a photograph. This is most obvious in nineteenth-

Katharine Hepburn, 1933.
Photographed by Ernest Bachrach for RKO. Here Hepburn is young, long, all angles and wide plains. She has just finished her first film, A Bill of Divorcement, *and the studio, excited but uncertain about the public's response, was promoting her as "Something New and Different"—an American Garbo. These early photographs were designed to glamourize character rather than physical beauty.*

century photographs, in which historical connotations of an image raise it above a photograph lacking such associations. There are many portraits of children of the nineteenth century, but if the photograph is by Lewis Carroll and the sitter the child who inspired him to write *Alice in Wonderland,* then we look longer and more intensely. If the form of the photograph were everything, a photograph of Veruschka would be the equivalent of one of Dietrich or Garbo. This is not the case. The reason goes deeper than the facile explanation that in the case of the film star we have her films to show us how she walked, talked, and handled herself in adversity, in victory, in love. The Hollywood portraits were able to convey an idea of the context in which these beings existed by the photographers' integration of form with the subject's own projection—a process comparable to, but independent of, the superb film vehicles created for the stars. Take, for example, a portrait of a now-forgotten star like Evelyn Brent. Without knowing anything about her life or having seen any of her movies, we respond to her photographs in a way that only a few of the celebrated artists of the previous decade (such as de Meyer) who photographed the stage and society beauties of their period had been able to make us respond to their sitters.

The same could also be said of most of the photographs of writers, poets, and statesmen one finds in exhibitions devoted to the work of the American-born pioneer Alvin Langdon Coburn (1882–1966) and the much-admired German-born Edwardian society photographer E. O. Hoppé (1878–1972). The unidentified images of Henry James, John Galsworthy, the young John Masefield, H. G. Wells, and others fail to give a clue to their work, nor do their photographs excite us to inquire further (with a few notable exceptions, such as G. B. Shaw, Theodore Roosevelt, and Mark Twain); but because of the reputations of the sitters, the images that were made of them are commonly applauded.

A full appreciation of the studio portrait photographers has been a long time in coming,* though they responded just as sympathetically and

---

*The Museum of Modern Art's 1978 appointment calendar, entitled *Faces,* shows for each week a reproduction of a painting, a sculpture, or a photograph, and a credit is given to the artist who created the work—except for the portraits of the Hollywood stars, for which the only credit given is to the Museum's Film Stills Archive. The calendar also features Andy Warhol's instant classic of Marilyn Monroe, which is merely his inspired laying-on of pop colors over the original photographic image, taken by Gene Kornman to publicize Monroe's role in *Niagara* (Fox, 1953). The Monroe is credited to Warhol without any mention of Kornman. The irony is compounded by the Museum's inclusion of this definitive example of the influence the work of these photographers has had on modern art and modern artists. The photographs in the calendar should be credited as follows: Carole Lombard by Eugene R. Richee (1932); Joan Crawford by George Hurrell (1931); Shirley Temple by Frank Powolny (1937); Greta Garbo by Ruth Harriet Louise (1927).

Evelyn Brent, 1926. Photographed by Henry Waxman. Waxman left his successful New York studio to open one in Los Angeles. His portraits of silent screen stars—among them Gloria Swanson, Pola Negri, John Gilbert, Mae Muray, and Norma Talmadge— were considered to be the most dramatic and were the most advanced of the era. Waxman's technical expertise and his fascination with the film personality, which he saw as exotic and extraordinary, resulted in photographs that brought new life to established careers and revealed the potential of unknown actors and actresses. When this portrait of Evelyn Brent was taken, her career was in trouble. She had appeared in a succession of fly-by-night productions as a gangster's moll and had become tagged as the Queen of the B's. After these photographs were released, she signed a contract with Paramount, became a major silent star, and starred in three of von Sternberg's films.

(Opposite) Norma Talmadge, 1924. Photographed by James Abbe.

(Above, left) Louise Brooks, 1929. Photographed by Edward Steichen.

(Above, right) John Barrymore, early 1920's. Photographed by Arnold Genthe. On the screen Barrymore projected hothouse romanticism. On the stage he was compelling, passionate, dynamic. This is a celebrated photographer's portrait of a handsome young man—perhaps a scholar or a poet or a banker. It is not a portrait that makes us see the larger-than-life passion or sweep that captivated the world on film.

worked with as much ingenuity as film directors and cameramen, who have long been singled out and honored for their contribution to the art of the twentieth century. Their photographs were given away to motion picture magazines, newspapers, and any fan who cared to write for one. Their work was seldom featured in the prestigious pages of *Vogue, Harper's Bazaar,* and *Vanity Fair* and consequently was not taken seriously enough in its own day. Nor was the treatment accorded their work within the studios likely to enhance their reputations. These images were printed and reproduced without the quality and the consummate technical understanding with which they had been taken—a control absolutely essential to the ideal print and relinquished for purposes of mass production. A day's work for a photographer was judged by weight instead of quality.* The images were sent out to be used and reused in books and magazines for decades after they were first printed, frequently painted over or touched-up by "foreign" (nonstudio) art departments. But for the past fifty years, in spite of the photo labs that have turned out hundreds, even thousands, of prints

* The Austrian portrait photographer Laszlo Willinger, who was signed by MGM in 1937 to replace George Hurrell, recalled the reaction of the head of the publicity department to his first day's work: "How many pounds of negatives have you done? Is that all you've shot today? This isn't heavy; usually we get two or three pounds of negatives."

from the same negative, these mass-produced glossies (for that is how we have become most familiar with them)—which have no correspondence to the original print—still seduce.

Periodically the New York magazines sent out their own photographers to Hollywood, and certainly Edward Steichen's, Arnold Genthe's, and Muky Munkacsi's portraits of stars were known and reproduced in photographic surveys. But the bulk of their work—of anonymous fashion models and now-forgotten Broadway personalities—is of little interest. Unavailable to Steichen and to visitors like Anton Bruehl, Genthe, George Hoyningen-Huene, and Cecil Beaton were the number of sessions, the amount of film, and the total commitment to the final portrait that was found only in the studios. No visiting photographer could compete with the long-term relationship that existed between the studio star and the studio photographer. At their best, what the visiting photographers took back to New York or London were portraits of a celebrity at a fixed moment in his or her career.

Their photographs were of people whose fame had in part been created by other photographs—those of the Hollywood studio photographers, men to whom their sitters' fame could only ever be a springboard to new heights and who had to devote every working day exclusively to this task. The studio photographers' acceptance of the mythology of the stars gave them the boldness the other photographers were rarely able to summon up. These outside photographers (who were poorly paid for their occasional "editorial" work—fashion and portraits—and supported themselves by doing advertisements) failed to understand and to convey the glory we so admired in the stars and thus left it to the Hollywood photographers to create the extraordinary work that captures the moment where one can see, for all future times, what had set these faces apart.

By 1910 the public's insatiable interest in stars, long and strenuously resisted by the penny arcade–minded film producers, who had already formed the Motion Picture Patent Co., gathered a momentum that could no longer be ignored by those wanting to survive as film-makers. The independent producers—treated as outlaws by the established trust producers—fought for survival. It was imperative that they always stay alert to the public's taste. While the autocratic trust continued to rule on the principle of mass production for mass distribution of a standard film, a fixed rental, and a daily change of program, the independents, coming from and working closer to the grass roots, realized that they might win by giving the public what it wanted and not, as the trust presumed, what they thought it needed. They noted the audience's preference for individual players, though the public's way of asking for its unidentified favorites was limited to requesting information about "this pretty girl" or "that handsome hero." The independent producers' observation led to the beginnings of star exploitation, although to be fair, those who launched it were as astounded as everybody else by the overwhelming success of the system they unleashed. Soon players in films made by the independents began to be advertised as stars, and an ever-growing legion of fans at last discovered that the golden-curled girl they had known as Little Mary was Mary Pickford.

The star system received its decisive boost in 1910. On April 1, a day for such occasions, newspapers splashed their front pages with bold headlines about the mysterious (presumed slain in St. Louis!) disappearance of the screen favorite the public loved but knew only as the Biograph Girl. The furor this news stirred up (before her reappearance a day or so later—safe, and soundly under new management to one of the independents) confirmed beyond any doubt that the star system was a *fait accompli.* Her new employers took ads to promote the former Biograph artist under her own name—Florence Lawrence—and, in another stroke of genius, sent her off to St. Louis to satisfy the city in which she was supposed to have died that she was very much alive. It was the first time that the film public had had an opportunity to see one of its favorites in person. At the station there was a stampede. In the city there were riots: Florence Lawrence had been booked to make two personal appearances in movie theatres belonging to her studio and was mobbed on the way to the first one. Her public showed their affection by tearing the buttons from her coat, the trimmings from her hat, and the hat from her head. She fainted. As an early example of Hollywood publicity, this personal appearance was a roaring success. A year later Florence Lawrence retired from films to raise roses.

After this incident it became clear that producers could not hope to flourish if they continued to ignore the public's desire for movie stars, and press agentry became an important aspect of creating and promoting them. The box-office value of the reams of free advertising in the nation's press, which had devoted pages to Miss Lawrence's disappearance and miraculous return from the jaws of death, ensured a succession of more outrageous stunts that would be developed and refined over the next decade.

Some of the early publicity men became celebrities in their own right because of their flamboyant stunts. One of these was Harry Reichenbach, who came from a background in circuses, fairs, magic acts, Broadway, and such. In 1913 he joined the fledgling Lasky company as their press agent and initiated the press book, an illustrated trade publication that accompanied each film as it was sent to the exhibitors, containing ads, plot summaries, and suggestions on how best to exploit the picture they had bought.* In 1914 Reichenbach went to work at Metro (so named because the company's president, on a first visit to Paris, saw the word all over town and liked it) and then spent the first year dreaming up ways to keep the new corporation's name in the news and the promised product in the exhibitors' minds while the company had as yet neither products nor ideas for any. In his posthumous autobiography, *Phantom Fame: The Anatomy of Ballyhoo,* Reichenbach wrote: "In the early stages we never appealed directly to the public, and the producer's selling force concentrated solely on the film distributors and the exhibitors. The publicity and advertising were of a special kind limited to

* The first press book was twelve pages long. In later years they reached up to one hundred pages and grew to the size of a table top. Today old press books are collector's items that sell in the four figures.

trade periodicals and correspondence. The press book was a typical device to this end." Of course, the interest created by his stunts attracted a far wider crowd than just distributors and exhibitors.

In America, the public that thronged to see a movie also enjoyed the publicity surrounding it. It was their reaction to the stunts at the box office that made the trade sit up. To promote one of his films, Reichenbach lodged a stuffed lion, four live apes, and the mysterious Prince Charley—an orangutan in a top hat and silk dress suit—in the foyer of a New York hotel to drum up publicity for one of the first Tarzan films. For an even duller sequel he concocted an even more outrageous stunt, smuggling a fully grown and quite live lion into a hotel room in a grand piano. The first clue to the room's resident came when the pianist asked room service for a lettuce sandwich, a glass of milk, and twenty pounds of raw meat.

A few years later Reichenbach got the New York City police to drag the lakes in Central Park for a missing Turkish virgin. Like all good publicity stunts, it had a happy conclusion—for the distributors. After the drama had been nationally syndicated for days, fed by rumors and the arrival of a secret high Turkish delegation* waiting in a New York hotel for news of her, she was found—not by New York's men in blue but by the proud papa, Universal, who celebrated her return with the national release of a fatted calf known as *Virgin of Stamboul* (1920)—for it was she who had been lost and was now found. The State of New York provided additional free publicity for the movie by passing a law forbidding the giving of false information to the press.

A similar approach taken over a longer period and devoted not to a film, which has an immediate but short-lived existence, but to a star, whose value could increase with the years, was a natural continuation for these methods. One of the most famous of these early exploits was the emergence of Theda Bara from the shadows of the sphinx to the shadows of the screen. She was the first film star made for films. Theodosia Goodman, a stage actress from Cincinnati, was given a new name—half contraction and half concoction—which her fans believed to be an anagram for "Arab Death"; a new background (her father was supposed to have been a roving French artist who met, loved, and left her mother, a mysterious Egyptian dancer); and a new, highly spiced image—exotic, mysterious, and as fatal as an asp.

The public's first glimpse of this smoldering Sheba came through

* Reichenbach had a few problems with his cast of V.I.P.'s, since the only Turks to be found in all New York were dishwashers and the like, who had to be trained in the ways of princes.

photographs, and these became an instrumental part in the creation of her image.* At that time there were no studio portrait photographers—not counting those cameramen, assistant cameramen, assistant directors, prop boys, grips, and others nearby who might take stills of scenes being shot. Bara was sent to one of New York's specialists in photographing stage stars, Underwood & Underwood. She spent days posing with skulls and crossbones, glass balls, "ancient" Egyptian sarcophagi presumed to contain the remnants of her noble ancestors, and all the other trademarks of Oriental mysticism that were to become the hallmarks of screen vamps.

But it was her ability to live up to the publicity that made Bara a star, not the publicity itself: on screen the privately demure young actress was everything the press agents had promised she would be. Her first starring role for Fox Film Corp., *A Fool There Was,* was the box-office hit of January 1915. Her popularity leapt ahead, and so did the men who were kept busy dreaming up and pounding out her publicity. The public enjoyed the stories for what they were—the more hair-raising and side-splitting, the better. Even articles suggesting that it was all a put-on didn't dampen their interest in her fabricated persona. Three overblown years at the top and over forty films (more than one a month)—not to mention the countless vamping imitators whose films came close on her trail—finally finished Bara's career. But by then her name had already become part of film lore.

Nineteen-fifteen was also the year Mary Pickford, who had begun working in films six years previously for five dollars a day, told her employers that she could no longer consider working for a mere ten thousand dollars a week. The following year she won a contract that guaranteed her $1.04 million a year—and perks. In the meantime she had signed an agreement with one of the largest newspaper syndicates to lend her name to a

---

* As soon as audiences knew the names of their idols, they started to collect pictures of them, and the rapid growth of the fan magazines—press books for the public—made photographs an ever-more important part of film-making. From the beginning the fan magazines promoted this interest, offering to sell their readers the photographs that appeared in their pages (*Motion Picture Story*, September 1913), ranging in price from 10 cents for plain, unmounted 4 × 5 prints to 50 cents for 10 × 12 prints to up to two dollars for mounted photos with hand-painted designs around the borders; later they even gave away "Splendid Sets of 80 4¼ × 8¼ unmounted, rotogravure portraits" as an inducement to buying a year's subscription to magazines like *Motion Picture* (April 1917). *Photoplay* was the most prestigious of the fan magazines and was justly famed for its brilliant rotogravure sections of star portraits. Beginning in 1916 and continuing into the twenties, it produced several hard-cover annuals consisting solely of over one hundred beautifully reproduced art portraits: "The First Book of Its Kind Ever Offered, 50 cents."

series of articles to be ghostwritten by her friend Frances Marion.* She also leased her idolized features to a maker of beauty creams, who promoted their product with large photo cutouts of Mary, not only bringing her additional revenues but enhancing her popularity by dreaming up the label "America's Sweetheart" for her.

The press reacted with glee to every bit of news connected with stars and movie-makers. The fact that most of it consisted of lies trumped up especially for them didn't seem to matter. After all, lies and hunches fueled ambitions and hopes—and they sold newspapers.

Theda Bara, 1918.
Photographed by Melbourne Spurr.

* Marion was one of the great Hollywood screenwriters and wrote many of Mary Pickford's films, as well as others, including *The Wind* (1928), *Anna Christie* (1930), *The Big House* (1930), *The Champ* (1931), *Dinner at Eight* (1933), and *Riffraff* (1936).

Conversely, newspapers helped to sell the stars. The furiously fought circulation wars took on a new direction when powerful press lords like William Randolph Hearst entered the film business to produce their own movies with their own stars, which would ensure them exclusive news. Newspapers also found themselves benefiting through the increasing film advertising revenue, and so they began to establish film review columns in their pages. In 1914 *Photoplay* magazine was launched, and with it a new, prosperous line of periodical publications based on the screen. It cost fifteen cents and averaged one hundred seventy pages, and its success was instantaneous. By 1925 its circulation had reached over half a million.

Studios were quick to draw their share from this connection with the press. By 1914 rapidly expanding film companies found themselves becoming something they had originally set out to avoid—programmed concerns dedicated to providing a consistent commercial supply. To compete successfully, they had to improve their product in both star value and production, and these films in turn required special selling and presentation above and beyond what had sufficed for the previous one- and two-reelers. To help recover costs for these increasingly expensive productions, which boasted high-priced star names and a growing use of foreign locations, a larger market was needed. To obtain greater control over distribution and outlets, film producers began buying movie theatres. When the Strand Theatre, with its nearly three thousand seats on two floors, opened on Broadway on April 11, 1914, it marked the movies' invasion of the very heart of theatre-land.* *Picture Play* reported in July 1916: "Movies are the fifth largest business in the U.S., and the only one that is not a manufacturer of essential goods. $575 millions have been the total invested in films for the year ending March 15, 1916. There are 18,000 theatres in the U.S., 25,200,000 people go to films each day. Movies employ 450,000 people."

Press agents—many of whose previous experience had been with circuses, theatres, or newspapers—were drawn to Los Angeles by the high salaries and soon became a necessary part of the studio machine: "If It's a Paramount Picture It's the Best Show in Town," "Selznick Pictures Make Happy Hours," and, a little later, "MGM—More Stars Than There Are in Heaven." It was only a small step from individual press agents to the setting up of entire publicity departments in the various studios.

* Standard theatre design called for three floors—orchestra, balcony, and gallery—and the seating capacity was usually six hundred to one thousand; the new movie palaces had only two floors, and their seating capacities ran from eighteen hundred to three thousand.

As the public's desire for stars grew, the studios succumbed and began making movies a star medium. The enormous influence Hollywood threatened to exert on the minds and manners of its consumers through the adoration of stars was beyond the comprehension of these girls and boys (which is what most of the stars were). They continued to behave and live much as individuals of similar background across the country might, with one very important exception: the sudden vast wealth brought by their popularity made it possible for them to realize their wildest private dreams. Of course, this made the stars enter even further into the public's consciousness, but it also made them conspicuous to other, less friendly observers. The self-appointed watchdogs of the nation's morals made it their business to monitor the private actions of the new idols and subjected them to a blistering scrutiny.*

Envy became the dark side of adulation. By 1917 movie-goers were informed that the Hollywood set had among its members two of the highest-salaried beings on the globe: Mary Pickford and Charles Chaplin. The public—who had made this situation possible—found it incredible that a curly-haired girl and a little funny man, with backgrounds no different from their own, could earn ten thousand dollars a week. But the public was so stimulated by these reports that they went in even greater numbers whenever a Pickford or Chaplin film appeared, just to *see* someone who earned that much money.

A tempest threatened to erupt at the divorce and subsequent remarriage of America's Sweetheart (Pickford) to America's Hero (Fairbanks). This powder keg defused itself because "love" was at the heart of the affair, the adoring public demonstrating that as long as life mirrored the fantasies of the screen, they would accept it. But there was nothing romantic about the scandals that surrounded comedian "Fatty" Arbuckle,† director William Desmond Taylor, and the nation's number-one heartthrob, Wallace Reid. Sex orgies, murders, and deaths from drug addiction did not provoke misty-eyed forgiveness. And once the lid was off, a steady stream of disclosures of salacious stories followed. Hollywood

---

* These professional reformers came into their own after World War I, though by then already more than a dozen states had set up censorship boards. No specific state or municipal censorship bureau monitored either the printed word or the theatre in the United States before the advent of motion pictures. And although both books and plays went much further in their use of sexually explicit images and frank language, censorship boards were set up in every state only for movies.

† Because of W. R. Hearst's desire to gain a foothold in the movie industry, his scandal sheets thoroughly exploited the Arbuckle tragedy; yet it was Hearst's mistress, Marion Davies, who later hired Arbuckle (working under a pseudonym) to direct *The Red Mill* (MGM, 1927), one of her lavish Hearst-financed vehicles.

replaced the fabled sin cities of the Bible in the nation's mind and soon was filled to bursting with correspondents from all over, assigned there by their newspapers to report the facts—or, if none were forthcoming, to make them up.*

The box-office returns on films starring the fallen idols and those linked to them (whether by fact or innuendo) showed a marked decline. Communities enforced strict and widely divergent new censorship laws, and church and civic groups insisted that offending films be withdrawn. The industry decided to take counteraction. In December 1921 the formerly antagonistic and otherwise competitive heads of studios united to form a solid righteous front, and approached one of the most respected pillars of the establishment—Postmaster General Will Hays—asking him to help them lead the industry back to decency and healthy box-office returns.

It was during these troublesome years that the value of an efficient and well-connected publicity department working for the studios' interest became more fully understood and appreciated. Publicity departments took on a new role: it became their function to ensure that nothing that might cause detrimental publicity to the end product occurred between the time of a movie's production and its release. If, despite all their precautions, something untoward did occur, the publicity department would see to it that the truth never reached the press, the public, or Will Hays.

It was only common sense for the studios to attempt to control their employees as much as possible. Moral clauses became standard in contracts: should a star receive any adverse publicity, the studio would have the right to cancel the contract immediately.† It was the publicity department's job to control whatever news reached the press about its studio and its stars, preferably by writing it themselves. If that was not convenient, they made sure that it was written by people who were beholden to them, and stars under contract were available for interviews only to correspondents of newspapers who were certain to be friendly.

This period also saw the beginning of the end of the successful private portrait photographers—men like Lansing Brown, Edward Thayer Monroe, Edwin Bower Hesser, Witzel, James Abbe, and Russell Ball—who had become internationally famous for their star portraits and rich by

* Hollywood was a boom town full of cowboys and shady ladies, who might work occasionally as extras in films. In the newspapers such a woman involved in her usual activity became a "Beautiful Film Star" and the cowboy on a weekend binge was a "Movie Hero Gone Wrong."
† There was no such clause indemnifying the stars against the studio; theoretically, at least, producers could not only have fun but could be seen to be having fun, without this affecting their careers.

Lillian Gish, 1923. The White Sister.
Photographed by James Albin.

selling them to magazines and newspapers. If a film company wanted to use their work, it had to pay for the prints like anyone else. But with the quantities of stills the studios now needed, it became evident that it would be cheaper to take the photographs themselves. Also, the studios wouldn't have to share credit with a photographer and would be able to create a look for their stars that would become associated in the public's mind with the particular studio that employed them.

Several of the existing Los Angeles photographic studios had worked on assignment for film studios, among them Witzel, for Fox, and Nelson Evans for Triangle and Sennett. In New York, studios and stars used Apeda, Underwood & Underwood, and Mishkin, Hoover. And certain perceptive stars like Lillian Gish and directors like Cecil B. DeMille were very much aware of the value of good still photographs in selling films to the public. DeMille employed many of the finest photographers —the already legendary Edward S. Curtis and Karl Struss among them— to take stills of his productions and the stars in them. Curtis worked on several of DeMille's films, including *Adam's Rib* (1923) and the silent *The Ten Commandments* (1923). For DeMille's last personally produced and directed film, a remake of *The Ten Commandments* (1956), the director had the famed Canadian portrait artist Karsh of Ottawa shoot a special series of the stars in character.

Lillian Gish's appreciation for quality portrait photography dated back to her days with Griffith, when Kenneth Alexander (later with United Artists and 20th Century) and James Abbe did many of his stills. Griffith had hired Abbe to shoot scenes as well as portraits for *Way Down East* (1920). He accompanied Lillian to Italy to shoot the stills for *The White Sister* (1923). In London he took stills and portraits of Dorothy Gish in her English productions. Dorothy's portraits for many of her films were done by Albin, New York's top theatrical photographer, including those for *The Bright Shawl* (1923) and *Romola* (1925). But most of the established portrait studios, as well as photographers lured to Hollywood by the beauty, fame, and wealth of the subjects before their lenses, preferred to enhance their reputations and pocketbooks by freelancing. This the studios now cracked down on.

The fact that few of the portrait photographers working in-house for the studios were men of renown like Abbe and de Meyer or giants like Steichen and Genthe proved no deterrent in the marketplace for which their work was intended. The newspapers and magazines clamored for the stills and portraits that the studios provided them free of charge in return for a caption that credited company and product. It was the subject matter that counted and not the person who photographed it, as the freelancers soon discovered. No matter how successful the work of these fine photographers had been, competition was now fierce, and with no movie stars to photograph, they returned East to photograph stage stars or went into fashion or advertising. Among the photographers who found themselves in this situation were Henry Waxman, who was responsible for the best known of Valentino's last portraits; Edwin Bower Hesser, who

Bessie Love, 1919. Photographed by Edwin Bower Hesser.

turned Griffith Park, rocks and all, into an Elysian Field for his studies of Grecian-robed stars such as Jean Harlow (see pages 52 and 53), Bessie Love , and Corinne Griffith; and Russell Ball, whose highly romantic close-ups of the silent screen stars, especially the women, anticipated the style to come.

By the end of the twenties, studio control was absolute. It reached from star to gateman and out of the studio across the country. Studios even went so far as to arrange marriages when they deemed it necessary to protect their investment. If it became known in the company that a certain popular male star was overtly homosexual, he was forced to marry to avert outside suspicion before it arose. This happened to some of the most famous romantic idols in the history of Hollywood. The same went for female stars with a preference for their own sex or (as with Kim Novak)

Jean Harlow, 1929. Photographed by Edwin Bower Hesser. Harlow is eighteen and has appeared as a dress extra in a number of Hal Roach's Laurel and Hardy comedies. These two photographs begin to reveal the qualities that would define Harlow as a star. You see a girl who is high-spirited, good-natured, erotic, and unashamed.

when they had boyfriends whose race, creed, or color was thought to jeopardize their star image. Pressure was put on magazines to discourage them from printing thought-provoking features about so-called ideal marriages in which the star lived in one house and the husband in another or about two bachelor actors who appeared to be sharing more than just an address.

Movie stars had to be above suspicion, their lives as flawless as their complexions. At MGM a network of studio spies was planted throughout the lot. Ted Allan, MGM portrait photographer, explained: "We didn't know who they were. Relatives in particular, interspersed among the staff, with different names, and they'd report back everything. There was a man in Central Casting whose brother—when he wasn't in a mental home—had small parts in almost every film, keeping his ears open for gossip. If he didn't hear anything, he'd make it up."

Other studios may have had—or soon would have—as many box-office names under contract, but it was MGM that established itself as the symbolic home of the Hollywood star. Many an overworked star on the Warner lot spoke enviously of the treatment MGM lavished on its stars. MGM accordingly directed all its impressive organization to promoting and sustaining this image.

The MGM publicity department in Culver City was headed by Howard Strickling, a former publicity man with Rex Ingram's studio in Nice. Highly departmentalized and with a staff of more than one hundred, it formed the most powerful non–film-producing unit on the lot. Tom Jones, a former Metro publicist, described it as "a three-hundred-and-sixty-five-days-a-year job. You never stopped, because you were working on pictures in production, pictures that were coming up, pictures currently in release, and also—always—on the stars assigned to you. Everything about them was news as far as you were concerned." Ted Allan, who gave up his own studio to become portrait photographer at MGM, said, "Later on, when I worked elsewhere, though I made more money I never felt as secure as I had at Metro."

Jones recalled the meetings the publicity department had twice a week to discuss personalities. "If we didn't have as much planted in the press as another studio did, we'd have to pull out all the stops, thinking up new layouts, new portrait sittings, just to create something different in a star's image that would make the papers, even if this meant revamping old campaigns." What had worked well with the silent-screen child star Jackie Coogan was adjusted for Jackie Cooper. When Marilyn Monroe came to MGM to make *The Asphalt Jungle* (1950), Eric Carpenter (see Notes on Other Photographers) photographed her in a pose and clinging dress similar to what he'd successfully used with Lana Turner, most of whose poses had been variations of those dreamed up for Harlow.

Publicity still photographer Bud Graybill (see Notes on Other Photographers) explained:

We'd write out our stills campaign and hand it in to Strickling for approval the same way writers would have to come up with ideas. If I were on a film in which they featured a fanciful sort of car, I might propose a feature on stars in their cars. Or stars with their pets. Some of the layouts could be quite novel. If the idea was cute and it was picked up, you'd get a million dollars' worth of free publicity, mentioning the studio and the film. One time I got Norma Shearer to pose with a rabbit. That really amazed Strickling.

Or I'd have them sitting outside their dressing rooms having lunch—Rainer, Shearer . . . eight or ten of them. Bingo. It was posed informality. When they weren't working, between pictures, we'd do things in their homes. I even had Shearer standing on her head, on a diving board. She was on location at Arrowhead, and I went up there with her to shoot some layouts. She came out early in the morning and had this Bible with her. "Good morning, Mr. Graybill." Very perfunctory. None of this "hello Frank, hello Bill." We shot some pictures of her like that, and then we said, "Let's go down to the lake." We were going to shoot her getting into a canoe, and as this lifeguard was helping her he laughed and said, "Gee, this is funny. We were doing this last week with Shirley Temple." She stepped out of the boat and said, "See you later, gentlemen." And that was the rest of the day's work gone. But these were pros. They knew their jobs and what was expected of them. The idea of these layouts was to keep them in the public's eye—to sell them in an attractive manner. The idea wasn't to get them with their guards down, scratching their butts, or looking dirty or unkempt.

Whatever was done was to enhance the star's image. As Loretta Young said, "I was never photographed in the kitchen. Ever. The reason was that it would have been asinine for me, and I'd tell them so in Publicity if they came up with an idea like that. The public knew I didn't cook. I'm a movie star. I don't know how to cook. I don't like to cook. I don't have time to cook. They knew I had a cook and a maid and a chauffeur and a butler. That's what all movie stars had. Sometimes when you start out you do silly things, like Garbo having to pose with that silly lion or with the Los Angeles track team. Everybody who sees it thinks it's silly. So why do it? That's why I decided as soon as I could I would never do things that didn't seem right for me."

Doing poster art at the studio was another way the publicity depart-

Norma Shearer, 1929. Photographed by Russell Ball. (For Shearer by Ruth Harriet Louise, see page 137; by George Hurrell, pages 217 and 219; by Laszlo Willinger, page 259.)

ment controlled things and got what they required. Laszlo Willinger, the celebrated Austrian photographer who was brought to MGM by Louis B. Mayer in 1937 and who photographed countless campaigns, pointed out: "The artists working in the advertising department would make rough sketches of the billboards, with the logo on it, and I had to fit my pictures into the existing format. The whole thing was planned precisely." The studio tried to take most of its portraits, advertising, and exploitation art *before* the picture ever started, so that when the cameras began to turn, the unit photographer could concentrate on shooting production stills and timely publicity art.

The several hundred stills that made up the key set for each major motion picture would be divided fairly evenly between gallery work and

set shots. They were broken down into seven basic categories: *straight portraits* (in street clothes, alone, in pairs, and in groups of leading players), *character portraits* (straight portraits but in costume), *advertising* (action plus character shots that are slightly broader in feeling than character portraits, so that they would be usable for poster and other outdoor advertising), *fashion* (women in styles—preferably adapted from those designed for the film—that may be in vogue when the film is released; the little Empress Eugénie hat that Garbo wore in *Romance* [see page 113] became a thirties fashion), *exploitation* (tie-in art in which a studio contract player poses with nationally advertised merchandise), *production* (actual scenes from the movie taken during the filming), and *publicity* (including art sometimes called informal or off-stage, strips, lay-

Evelyn Brent, 1929. Photographed by Russell Ball. Ball was one of the most successful independent photographers of the twenties. His portraits were glamorous, sensual, and dreamy. Until the studios opened their own galleries, virtually every star came to his studio on the Strip for portraits.

outs, gag ideas—like the ones Bud Graybill described above—seasonal stunts, montages, and so on).

A campaign meeting was called before every picture was begun. There might be eight films in production at once, and one publicist and two assistants were assigned to each. Someone responsible for putting the campaign together would be there from the photography department to ask questions. What's the film about? Are the costumes going to be of particular interest? The sets? How's the star going to look? The meetings covered magazine and newspaper stories—what photos, spreads, and off-stage portraits were to be used to sell the film.

At the smaller studios there was more give-and-take between departments. Bob Coburn ran the photo department and took the portraits for Goldwyn in the thirties (in 1941 he took over at Columbia) and was involved in every aspect of selling: "I'd read the script and get an idea of what to concentrate on. Then I'd go on the set and shoot what I felt was necessary. At Goldwyn I was in complete charge of my department. Goldwyn wanted it that way. If, on occasion, *Life* would want a cover shot of Gary Cooper, I'd shoot it. Goldwyn kept track of all publicity."

Once the copy for a campaign was approved, it was sent to the planting department. Five people did nothing but place stories in newspapers and magazines; these had some factual basis but were generally puff pieces. "People believed and bought tickets on the basis of what fan magazines had to say," explained William Walling. The "planters" worked closely with the editors and would get them to use photographs of up-and-coming stars in return for exclusive photographs of established stars. Ideal Publications put out five or six fan magazines for which the studio's portrait gallery was always taking photographs.

In addition to portraits, studios also had to think of layout and off-stage art, for which they had their own publicity photographers to cover outside studio events, such as premieres and conventions. There were also photo services like Globe and Black Star that employed a staff of photographers who did nothing but cover the nightclub circuit. Though not employed by them, they had to abide by certain rules set down by the studios. One of these was that no matter where they might be, female stars were never to be photographed with a drink or a cigarette. They had to be just as careful to take the drink off the table and remove the cigarette from the star's hand even if the stars themselves couldn't have cared less, because the photographers knew that the studios would object. There is a famous wartime photo of Lana Turner with her hand raised and fingers parted in what was captioned as her V for Victory salute. In fact, she had been about to inhale a cigarette, and her gesture,

with the offending cigarette retouched out, suggested something the Allies might have enjoyed more than sympathy. As far as the public was concerned, the female stars drank cocoa and ate candy.

A publicist's job could also be precarious. Tom Jones told this story:

We had a girl under contract, Linda Christian, who was very voluptuous and stunning to look at, with copper-red hair. Someone in publicity suggested we call her the "Anatomic Bomb" girl. She was going to be the new epitome of sex. We'd had "Oomph," "It," "The Body," and "Ping!" so they decided this would be a good catch phrase for Linda. Bob Landry [who created the marvelous

Clara Bow, 1921. Photographed by Nickolas Muray. Bow is eighteen here. A year before she had won a "Fame & Fortune" contest sponsored by three fan magazines. The prize: a screen test and a small part in a film.

Clara Bow, 1926. Photographed by Eugene R. Richee. A few years later. Bow has become Paramount's biggest draw. This portrait was made to promote her new movie, It *(1927).*

Life picture of Rita Hayworth in a negligee] thought she was sensational and promised to try to create something special with her. I was handed the assignment because I had been working with Linda, so she trusted me. Bob wanted her to wear something very sexy. I picked out a negligee that Lana Turner had worn—chiffon over a silk slip, with braiding on the shoulders and cut low at the front. Bob posed her against the open door of a bedroom but felt that something was wrong with the whole setup—something to do with the lighting. Linda agreed, left the room, and returned having removed her silk underslip so that she was wearing only the chiffon part. This, of course, was completely see-through. It was perfect for what Bob wanted, but I was worried. If it came out too sexy, I could lose my job. Bob assured me that he would be careful and that if there were any photos the studio objected to he would kill the sitting. So before showing them to anyone else he took them to the MGM photo editor, who thought they were beautiful, and they okayed the pictures for release.

If Jones's caution seems excessive, it was firmly grounded in an earlier mistake that had almost cost one studio photographer his job and had an adverse effect on the career of the popular musical star Carmen Miranda. Frank Powolny, a pioneer still man at Fox since the twenties (and one of their leading portrait photographers from the mid-thirties on, when he was Loretta Young's favorite photographer), could smile when he told me the story, since he survived the fiasco, but even forty years later, he still regretted it.

I was briefly fired because of a shot I took of Carmen being lifted into the air with her skirt flying up over her hips. I took it on a Saturday, August 11 or 12. I was going to go away on my vacation and had to get some work done before then. So I told Cesar [Romero], who was on the lot rehearsing a number, to get Carmen over to the gallery so that I could shoot some art on them for the film [*Weekend in Havana,* 1941]. She was relaxing in the dressing room after lunch when Cesar told her, "Come on, Frank's waiting to take some pictures before he leaves." And she said, "Okay, fine." Everything was set up. They were going to go through a dance number, with people standing about watching, and me with my brand-new Speed-Graphic Graflex with the flash. Nobody there seemed to notice anything unusual, and I was busy watching Carmen's and Cesar's faces. I think I shot her at one four-hundredths of a second. I sent the results off to the lab and went on my vacation. When I came back two weeks later the fellows came up to me and said, "By the way, Frank, remember those pictures of Carmen Miranda? Why don't you go up to your office and look at them." I discovered that I had taken a shot of Carmen without her undies. You could see everything. Somebody in the stills department had stolen the print when it was being developed and made two prints of it and showed it to a friend, who went to a third party, who made a dupe negative, and so on. It was a big incident at the time. The studio destroyed the original negative, but by then the copies were everywhere. Carmen was furious with me. She wanted to sue me, but then she dropped the case, and I was only fired for a brief time. Of course, you couldn't print it in magazines; it was just circulated privately.

Whether or not it seriously affected Miranda's career is hard to say now, but word of it went even further than the photograph itself, and people's image of Miranda altered. Twentieth Century-Fox, which had been grooming her for stardom, finished up her contract by using her as a still-volatile but distinctly second-string comedy figure in support of their crop of golden-haired leading ladies. It was quite likely that Powolny got back his job because of the wartime shortage of good photographers rather than because he had been with the studio for over twenty years or because the photograph had been an honest mistake.

What the publicity department might overlook, the Motion Picture Producers and Distributors Association, under the direction of the Hays office, was sure to catch. Anything shot in the studio had to go to them for final approval. Censorship, especially after the tightening of the Production Code in 1934, was very strict. When Lucille Ball played a nightclub dancer in *Easy to Wed* (1946), a remake of Jean Harlow's *Libeled Lady* (1936), she had a scene in which her costume was hitched up on one side with a garter over her stocking. You were not supposed to show flesh above the stocking tops, and in spite of the fact that her stocking went beyond the garter, everything above the garter, including the stocking, still counted as flesh, so in all the stills the garter had to be touched out and the net stockings painted in.

Some photographers used certain ploys to try to get around the censorship to some extent. As Madison Lacy (see Notes on Other Photographers) explained, "You'd deliberately make some things more erotic than others. They'd kill the most erotic ones, and you'd still have some that were reasonable by comparison."

Laszlo Willinger, who photographed nearly all the great stars on two continents—Dietrich, Isa Miranda, Emil Jannings, Brigitte Helm, Zarah Leander—said that when he got to Hollywood, you couldn't show cleavage. "There was a whole group of retouchers at every studio who did nothing but take the cleavage out of breasts. In those days the stars had one breast that stretched from shoulder to shoulder, creating a new breed of cyclops-chested women. You couldn't show the inside of a thigh. Have you ever tried to photograph a dancer and not show the inside of a thigh?

You can't. When you shot doubles, there were very strict rules. For instance, in clinches the man always had to be higher than the woman, because it wasn't considered nice otherwise. The men had to wear ties and jackets. And if you shot a man in bathing trunks or a gymnasium outfit, there couldn't be any unseemly bumps, and the body hair had to be retouched."

This wasn't such a problem in the years when the only man on the screen without his shirt and tie was Tarzan. But with the advent of pirate pictures, bare chests became commonplace, and hirsute male stars like John Payne and William Holden had to undergo the indignity of shaving their chests. Navels were another no-no and had to be removed from shots of women in two-piece bathing suits. The public didn't voice any objections to these anatomical reconstructions. Having accepted movie stars as a breed apart, perhaps this suggestion of their virgin birth merely confirmed it.

A still is a photograph taken with a hand-held camera of a scene being filmed—as opposed to a frame blow-up, which is a print made from the film itself—and used to promote a movie. The long exposure time required by the early cameras meant that everyone had to stay perfectly motionless while the photograph was being taken; hence, the term "still." The still men, as these photographers became known, were actually often the most active workers on the lot.

Many of the best-known portrait photographers—Ernest Bachrach, Clarence S. Bull, Otto Dyar, Robert Coburn, Gene Kornman, Eugene R. Richee, Ray Jones, William Walling—came from the ranks of the early still men, having initially been taken on as part of the movie camera crew. And as anyone who has ever glanced through an old Hollywood fan magazine—or its current reincarnation, Hollywood histories or biographies—knows, moving pictures may have made the film industry, but stills kept them alive. The infancy of the movie industry was an exciting, vital time, perfectly suited to the hardy pioneer spirit of men equipped with a flair for invention and improvisation as well as a reckless disregard for life and limb. The pioneers were a heterogeneous group of first-, second-, and third-generation Americans and more recent immigrants from Europe. They worked as directors, performers, news photographers, stonemasons, painters, and—most important of all—behind the cameras. As the business grew up, functions became more defined, unions were organized, and those directly involved in the production of a film began to be accorded the respect and wages dictated by the importance of their jobs. However, those responsible for one of the greatest jobs of photographic salesmanship in history—the men who shot the stills—were shunted aside, regarded as little more than a nuisance—albeit a necessary one. Few people on the set even knew their last names.

Nor did the primitive equipment they had to work with make things easier for them. By 1937 the movie camera, benefiting from continual scientific and technical advances, had sharper lenses, used supersensitive film, and permitted greater flexibility. But the bulky 8 × 10 still camera—the most important piece of equipment in studio portrait work—had hardly altered. The portrait view camera on its tripod in Ray Jones's gallery at Universal in 1937 was the same model that Walling and Richee had used at Paramount in 1932, that Powolny had used at Fox in 1924, and that Madison Lacy had begun taking stills with for Griffith in 1917. And the still photographer was expected to convey motion with this cumbersome 8 × 10 Eastman or Agfa Ansco view camera, equipped with a 10- or 12-inch Goerz Dagor f6.8. lens (virtually unchanged since 1917) or the somewhat smaller 5 × 7 and 4 × 5 Graphic Graflex, which was used for action work and sporty shots because of its faster speed (it also required a tripod).

Until shortly after World War I, photographers had to carry around with them on location not only their cameras but also the heavy and fragile orthochromatic glass plates. A dozen of them weighed as much as the cut film negatives for the entire picture. Shortly after the war, the Eastman laboratory brought out a new high-speed emulsion that they rolled out on a sheet of celluloid instead of glass. The new negatives weren't much faster, but at least they were a lot lighter.*

Another major improvement was the introduction of supersensitive still film, though this did not occur until around 1930. The vastly less sensitive film used earlier, such as the Eastman panchromatic cut film, was about 60 percent slower than the supersensitive motion picture film, for which the set was lit and the actors made up. This meant that the still photographer—already under pressure from irritable crews waiting to strike the set and from actors between takes and thus nervous—was compelled to double or triple his already longer normal exposure (approximately 1.5 seconds) to ensure that the still image would be sharp and would possess the admired depth of the filmed image. And even with this increased exposure time, the difference in the sensitivity characteristics of film and still emulsions was such that it was impossible to produce the same lighting effects and contrast that the cinematographers would get. Shooting action required that the photographer wait for a pause in activity before pressing the plunger. The hand had to be quick to stop

* Ira Hoke, reminiscing in "Some Historical Facts," *International Photographer* (March 1941). Hoke was the still man on many of the Jack Hoxie and Buck Jones Westerns at Fox, and later at Republic Pictures, where he worked on most of the Gene Autry and Roy Rogers films.

the action at such a slow shutter speed.* With so many handicaps and so many tempers to contend with, the job of still photographer clearly required men of initiative, adaptability, strength, a sense of humor, imagination, and a thick skin.

A measure of recognition was accorded them in 1932, when Harry Cottrell, head of Paramount's stills department, acknowledged the contribution of his department, which he described as the right arm of the publicity department. The previous year they had supplied close to a million stills to syndicated newspapers and magazines all over the world. This is even more impressive when one considers that this figure represented the work of two portrait photographers—Eugene R. Richee in Gallery 1 and William Walling in the smaller gallery—and four publicity and production still photographers—Gordon Head (*Night After Night*, 1932), Don English (*Dishonored*, 1931; *Shanghai Express*, 1932; *The Scarlet Empress*, 1934; *The Devil Is a Woman*, 1935), Sherman Clark (*A Farewell to Arms*, 1932), and Mack Elliott (*Tonight Is Ours*, 1933). Among them, they averaged approximately two hundred fifty negatives a day, of which one-third would be usable. The breakdown of materials used was as follows: fifty-four thousand 8 × 10 negatives, twelve thousand 4 × 5 negatives, five tons of hypo, two thousand pounds of sodium sulphate, and other ingredients in proportion.

The figures for the Warner Bros. still department in 1933 are similarly imposing. They had about thirty employees connected with the photography department under Gene O'Brien. In addition to the photographers there were the retouchers, developers, printers, and laboratory technicians. Elmer Fryer† was the chief portrait photographer at the studio from 1930 to 1940, and Scotty Welbourne† had the other gallery. (For two years, between 1938 and 1940, George Hurrell had his own gallery at the studio as well.) The still and publicity photographers included Madison Lacy, Bert Six (who took over the Warner Bros. gallery after Welbourne left in 1945 and was Bette Davis's favorite photographer, shooting stills for *Jezebel*, 1938; *Juarez*, 1939; *Dark Victory*, 1939; *The Letter*, 1940; *Now Voyager*, 1942), and Bert "Buddy" Longworth† (*Footlight Parade*, 1933; *Gold Diggers of 1933*; *Dames*, 1934; *Wonder Bar*, 1934; *Anthony Adverse*, 1936; *The Sea Hawk*, 1940). These photographers averaged three hundred stills a day during a normal production—

---

* According to Fred Hendrickson, who started out in 1915 as an assistant cameraman with the Kalem Co. in Jacksonville, Florida, when "the first cameraman was director of photography, operative cameraman, and still man."
† See Notes on Other Photographers.

and this does not include photographs taken in the gallery or at portrait sittings. From these three hundred negatives the lab workers turned out about fourteen hundred prints, not counting the enlargements (11×14 and 16×20 prints) required by some periodicals. For example, on *Dames* more than a thousand usable still photographs were taken; on *Madame Du Barry* (1934), more than seven hundred.

Lacy described what it was like to be a still man during the early days of Hollywood, circa 1916–17: "When I first started out, you handled slates, loaded cameras, timed the shots, fero-tagged the fero-tag tin, dried the prints, loaded, made copies. We had to develop our own prints, which we did in a piro soup that made our hands as black as coal, because on the set you don't always have the lights you like, so in your printing you learned to burn in something that's very hot or hold back something when there isn't enough light. You also had to do your own retouching. Anything at all that had to be done, you did."

When Lacy started out, the still man also assisted the director and the cameraman in their work. But by 1924 the demands for his services as a photographer had increased to such an extent that these other responsibilities were dropped. When a picture was in preparation, it was the still man's job to scout for suitable locations and to bring back photographs of the various sites for the director to choose from. He photographed practically every valuable piece of studio property, so that when a set required a specific type of door or window or a particular style of sofa or wedding cake, the technical director could go to his file of stills and locate it. The still man was required to shoot the stars in both costume and makeup so that if a scene had to be reshot on another day, the still could be used as reference to ensure that they would look the same. (Later on, the makeup men would work from stills taken of each actor and actress at the outset, so that they would be able to keep the shading and the shadows on the star's face consistent from day to day.)

As the other departments became better manned, with assistants and assistant assistants, and functions within them sharply defined, the still photographer continued to lug his own cumbersome cameras and slide holders to any locale the assignment might demand, from Arctic wastes to African jungles. (While the modern photojournalist probably carries as much weight—what with five or six 35 mm. cameras, fifteen lenses, and all the equipment that goes with them, including the most up-to-date light meters—he has people to help him, and the equipment itself simplifies his task to an enormous degree.) The general impression was that a still man had to focus the camera and time the negative. However, these were actually only details. He had to know how to group his sub-

Mary Astor, 1939. Photographed by
A. L. ("Whitey") Schaefer.

jects, avoid blank spaces, and feature the leading players without making it too obvious. This grouping sometimes necessitated changing a light or two, and he also had to direct the actors in what he wished them to do.

And, of course, he was always trying to get some good shots of the stars. With some of the high-strung talents, this could be tricky. Frank Powolny explained how Constance Bennett would say, "Don't bother me now, Frank. We'll get it later." "Only there never was a later," he said. "So I would just forget about her and would go ahead and do the others. Of course, when the stills were brought down to the set and

everyone looked at them, she asked me where she was in them, and I told her that she had asked me not to bother her with it and I hadn't. Of course she would be furious."

But usually stars were more cooperative. They understood what was expected of them and would go out of their way to help. Katharine Hepburn commented: "I used to pose for them in the scene and off the set because of my interest in stills. Otherwise the poor man on the set, they'd be telling him, 'Oh, for God's sake, you don't want a still of that! We can't wait for a still.' But I always used to encourage the still man and I'd protect him."

Clark Gable, 1932.
Photographed by Otto Dyar.

Anna May Wong, 1932.
Photographed by Otto Dyar.

Time was always a factor. "They didn't like to see a second wasted anywhere along the line," Powolny said, "so you had to know what to do long before you made your exposure. And you had to be right the first time. You didn't get a chance for retakes—not on those big outdoor pictures like *The Big Trail* [Fox, 1930]. I was the only still man there and had to keep up with nine or ten movie cameras, because this was one of the first movies shot in 'grandeur vision'—what they later brought back and called Cinerama. Some of those scenes, like the buffalo drive, were real killers—there's no posing a herd of buffaloes! And I had to do this with the standard 8 × 10 portrait camera. At the same time, I also had to

Gary Cooper, 1937. Photographed by William Walling, Jr., for Paramount. Walling understood actors—his parents were actors and he himself had acted in silent films. He also understood the camera—he had worked as an assistant movie cameraman with John Ford, whose suggestion it had been that Walling concentrate on stills. In 1932 Walling took over one of the portrait galleries at Paramount, where he photographed many of the studio's younger stars.

remember that these pictures were going to be reproduced in magazine and newspaper cuts, so you couldn't go in too much for delicate gradations or extreme high-key or low-key effects. The equivalent for a cameraman would be if he would have to remember while filming that the release prints were going to be made of bad dupes and poorly projected. And always you had to keep in mind that the stills you took had to tell a story, so there had to be a definite idea behind each one, and the composition had to be perfect every time—or you'd hear about it from the publicity department." As Al St. Hilaire (see Notes on Other Photographers) explained, "The magazines would never give us any complaints about our prints being too dark or whatever. The complaints came from publicity. Some studios were really absurd about seeing everything. Over at Fox they complained because they couldn't see the buttons on a man's clothes. They wanted to see buttons!"

The still man was supposed to do all this in practically the time it takes to place the camera in position, focus, and snap the exposure. If he took longer, the director was apt to become impatient. Not many of them were like Frank Borzage, Cecil B. DeMille, and F. W. Murnau, taking as active an interest in the stills as in every other aspect of their films. Powolny recalled that Murnau "always took special pains to check up on the composition of his stills, just as he did on his movie shots. He realized the value of getting the camera in exactly the right place. He would look through my camera, and if he thought the composition could be improved, he would suggest moving the camera—say, an inch or two one way or the other—instead of doing as so many of them did, saying, 'Hurry up, shoot the darn thing!' But these were the exceptions."

To get the shots they wanted, the Hollywood photographers took tremendous risks, and their resourcefulness was second to none. James Manatt (for over two decades one of the top still men at MGM, where he worked on a number of Garbo's films and later became the favorite of Katharine Hepburn) was responsible for the stills on *The Trail of '98* (1928), for which he froze fingers and toes to get the stark, chillingly beautiful snow scenes in Alaska and on the Continental Divide, in such spots as the Chilkoot Pass. Arthur Marion, a former newspaperman, was at his best on action stories and thrillers. He once walked twenty miles over mountainous terrain to get a vista shot of a Wyoming prairie for a Tim McCoy Western, which rivals anything Edward S. Curtis ever did.

Ducking around the sets as unobtrusively as possible, the still photographer followed the production—even, like Daniel, into the lion's

Gloria Swanson, 1919, Male and Female *(Famous Players–Lasky). Photographed by Karl Struss. Struss was already an established portrait photographer when he came to Hollywood to work as a cameraman. He began by taking stills for Cecil B. DeMille on* Male and Female *"as a means of getting into the film business. During the war I'd looked at two films a night at a dime apiece and I could see that they didn't have many photographers. I'd already had four years' experience of photography, as well as taking over Clarence White's studio in New York from 1914 to 1917, so I felt there'd be an opening for me in films.*

"DeMille would look through the still camera lens and realize that I knew something about composition, so he put me on as third cameraman. In those early stills it was difficult to be creative because you had people moving, and when they posed it was pretty conventional. Although DeMille was one of the new school of directors, his background was theatre, so everything was set. Long shot, people come in, cross the set, exit. For me the composition was in the camera, whether I was shooting a photograph or a film."

*Struss became one of the industry's foremost cinematographers (*Sparrows, *1926;* Sunrise, *1927;* The Sign of the Cross, *1932;* Island of Lost Souls, *1933).*

Photograph printed by Ted Allan, 1980.

den. Said Karl Struss, who began his career in Hollywood as a still photographer for DeMille's *Male and Female* (Paramount, 1919), "To shoot the picture of Gloria Swanson and the lion, I went down into the pit with my 8 × 10 camera and my low camera tripod, because I had to work from a static position to be able to open the lens enough to get enough light in the composition. Then I had to close the shutter, put the plate holder in, and pull the slide. I had to set the shutter and give it an exposure of about one second and a half, stop down to sixteen, put the slide in, get the camera out. They are also shooting the scene for the film through a hole in the bars of the cage, and the whole time Gloria was lying there, with the lion on her back. DeMille was standing outside with a gun in his hand trained at the lion in case anything should go wrong and was more scared than she was."

The fantasy classic *King Kong* (RKO, 1933) is justly famed for its deft blending of miniature, animation, and live action. Of course, there could be no action stills of scenes involving the animated Kong with the human cast, but the stills that have survived are superbly crafted. Bob Coburn was assigned to the film by Ernest Bachrach ("the man who taught me more about photography than any other human being") and explained, "When I made those montage stills for *King Kong*, I'd cut out a line and not have it show, so you could print those things in it with very little retouching. It would look just like it was a scene out of the film. Of course, we'd photograph the models for Kong, so that we'd know where we were going to put Fay Wray, whether in his hand or somewhere else. The picture took a couple of years to make. We asked them to call up our department every time they changed to an interesting shot of Kong, and I'd go down there. Sometimes I'd stay all day if it was an interesting setup, shooting him every kind of way."

Until the still men formed themselves into a union (Local 659, founded in August 1928), "the studios really abused us all," said Ed Estabrook, long-time union president. "We had to work up to twenty-four-hour shifts, there were no vacations, there was no overtime; we were required to work from the early daylight hours to the last possible minute of shooting light, and this could include Sundays as well if you were on location and shooting fell behind schedule." *

With the work so demanding and the praise so sparse (an attitude that did not change with the formation of the union), why did the still

* Estabrook left New York in 1920, three years later becoming first cameraman with Techni-color Motion Picture Co., where he shot the color sequences for *Ben-Hur* (1926), DeMille's *The King of Kings* (1927), and *The Broadway Melody* (1929).

Charles Boyer, 1937. Photographed by Robert Coburn for Goldwyn. Coburn grew up on a cattle ranch in Montana. He arrived in Hollywood when he was sixteen and shot the stills on hundreds of B Westerns. His break came when he went to work at RKO as Ernest Bachrach's assistant: "Bachrach taught me the fundamentals, from lab work on. He taught me never to take a straight shot. We always cocked our cameras. We would either sit on our butts and shoot up, or turn the camera, rather than take what we called 'the company front.'" Coburn's Charles Boyer is the Boyer the public wanted to be seduced by. It is the American view of the European male— sophisticated, cynical, provocative, dangerous. With women, the photographer could suggest eroticism through costuming and highlights on bared shoulders; with men, the area was limited to the face—the curve of the forehead, the eyelids, the hands.

men do it? Many of them could have gone on to become more highly regarded—not to mention better paid—as camera operators, directors, or actors. When Madison Lacy joined Griffith in 1917, he received twelve dollars a week. By 1923 the average salary for a still photographer was thirty-five dollars a week; only a few made as much as forty-five. (To give an idea of the purchasing power of the dollar in those days, the price of the Ford economy car was two hundred sixty-five dollars.) By 1933 the still photographer's salary had reached seventy-five dollars a week.

Yet for all the drawbacks, the Hollywood still photographers remained some of the most independent men in the industry. Although the publicity department (and even, in a sense, the production department) was above them, as long as they satisfied the needs of the studio and the magazines, they could shoot whatever they wanted. On location they were their own directors and their own cameramen, and they themselves determined what they would photograph.

Powolny commented, "They used to say that still men were disappointed cameramen, but I don't think so. I've known too many good still men who were just as good with a movie camera and who, like me, preferred still work. In my case, I suppose, it had a lot to do with my early training in painting and sculpture; there is the same problem—suggesting motion and telling a story in a fixed pattern of light and shade."

In 1978, shortly before his death, Madison Lacy told me, "When I went into motion-picture photography, I didn't enjoy it as much as taking stills. There were too many people saying what they wanted you to do, and you couldn't leave the camera. So I went back to still photography. There you were free. There you were your own man."

Robert Coburn headed the portrait gallery for Goldwyn beginning in 1935 and then in 1941 went to Columbia. His passion for the camera also began when he was a child. "You either have the feeling for it or you don't," he said. "I've had men working for me when I was in charge of the stills department who were scared to death to go on a set and take a picture because they were frightened of working for a man like Jack Ford, who just hated having photographers around. (He hated his cameramen, too.) Now I was trigger happy. You couldn't keep me away from a set." The medium enthralled these pioneers of photojournalism.

We know that the photographic works of the early still men influenced the portrait photographers years later. As Louise Brooks, silent-film actress and film historian, commented after viewing the 1978 exhibition of Richard Avedon's work at the Metropolitan Museum of Art in New York, "How powerfully his long shots have been influenced with

Merle Oberon, 1937, Beloved Enemy *(Goldwyn). Photographed by Robert Coburn. "The idea for this session was something I dreamt up during a lull in shooting, when they ran into some difficulty filming Merle."* Coburn explained. *"She wasn't wearing much makeup when I took the picture. Actually, I didn't like it when they wore too much, and besides, I could cover any problems with lighting. She was still recuperating from makeup poisoning, which had scarred her face, and she couldn't wear makeup to disguise it. I figured out that if you lit her flat, nothing would show. The cameraman on this film, faced with the problem of how to shoot her close-ups, saw what I was doing and used the same lighting setup."*

action and a story by the still photographer's camera, set up to the left of the movie camera, photographing the action as it happened during the shooting of a scene truly alive—not 'scene stills' reconstituted after the day's filming."

Less well known, however, is the influence the still photographers had on the movies themselves. Clarence S. Bull, for over forty years head of the MGM stills department, believed that the work of his men paved the way for photographic effects that were later picked up by movie cameramen. He cited several cases:

Milton Browne is responsible for the beautiful still photography in the Lillian Gish pictures, and his camera effects have served in a number of cases to set new precedents for the screen. Wallace Chewning forsook the ranks of motion picture cameramen to become a still photographer, approaching his task with the comprehensive knowledge of screen requirements and the idea of using still photography in aiding the film effects of the pictures. On the Lon Chaney picture *London After Midnight* [1927], he passed weeks of study, using the script and light effects to devise methods of translating fear in terms of photography. Chaney's picture was a thriller, with the star as a detective in a strange mystery in a haunted house. It naturally lent itself to fantastic shadows and weird effects.

The portraits that New York photographer Hendrick Sartov took of Lillian Gish so impressed her and D. W. Griffith that the director hired him to shoot several close-ups of Gish which were then inserted into the already completed film *Hearts of the World* (1918). The stills shot for the romantic-looking billboards used for advance publicity on *A Farewell to Arms* (1932), starring Helen Hayes and Gary Cooper, so impressed the film's director, Frank Borzage, that when he shot the film's love scenes, he used the stills as a guide. The Hollywood studio portrait photographers of the late twenties influenced the overall visual style of the films of the thirties, for it was clearly apparent in the portraits long before it was on the screen. By the early thirties the portrait photographers were so highly regarded by the stars and the producers that they were often consulted when it came time to shoot the stars' close-ups for the screen.

By 1928, the term "still photographer" covered a multitude of functions, all of which could be done by the same man. With the formation of their union in 1928, not only were their jobs guaranteed and salaries raised, but their functions became more clearly defined; what had already become the practice at many studios was now stated officially. At the smaller studios, of course, the head of the stills department would take the portraits and do special work on films, including advertising tie-ins and even unit photography. This continued to be the rule at independents like Goldwyn, Walter Wanger, Selznick Pictures, and Alexander Korda Productions, as well as the smaller studios like Republic. But by the end of the decade at the major studios—Warner Bros., 20th Century-Fox, Paramount, RKO, Universal, and of course MGM—portrait photographers, in some cases as many as two or three, were working exclusively on portraiture.

Before the studios set up gallery space and lighting equipment on the lot, a still photographer would create his own makeshift gallery wherever he was working—in a canvas tent or beneath leafy trees if he were on location, or in the shadow of a sound stage. Stills were taken between

Louise Brooks, 1928. Photographed by Eugene R. Richee; kimono designed by Travis Banton. Brooks was a rising star whose individuality would cost her her career, but not before she had starred in Beggars of Life *(1928),* A Girl in Every Port *(1928),* Pandora's Box *(1929), and* Diary of a Lost Girl *(1929). In this photograph, one of several hundred taken during her years as one of Paramount's most promising contract artists, Richee captures her personality—tough, abrasive, but, even at her spikiest, adorable. She sits, supple and lithe as a cat, regarding the world. She seems to be listening with her eyes.*

setups or after a long day's shooting, when a star would not be in the mood for much more standing about. When a still photographer was working on a closed set, to get enough light on the stage for their lenses, the stage doors were opened and a white reflector was used, because the early power-speed film was too sensitive to blue and would have created far too much contrast on a closed stage. The Cooper-York lighting then in use was rather primitive, the arcs sputtering and often dying just as everything was at last ready, and the effect was that of neon lighting. The mercury content of the arc lights added a harsh bluish tone that tended to age the actors and actresses, who wore a very heavy white makeup to compensate. Even so, hot spots and dark rings always seemed to be in the wrong places, and many times they wouldn't be noticed until they showed up on the negatives. Another problem of the old arc lights— the big heavy sunspots and overhead floods—was the damage they did to the eyes. For all these reasons the still men tried to take their portraits outside, using natural reflected light from the sky.

It was at Famous Players–Lasky (later Paramount), the largest of the early studios, that the first, albeit rudimentary, gallery was set up in 1920 or 1921, at the suggestion of their still photographer, Donald Biddle Keyes (see Notes on Other Photographers). This gallery was used for advertising art—better known as poster art. As soon as the players received their finished costumes, they were photographed against a plain or otherwise suitable background in scenes from the movie. The star gazing furtively over his or her shoulder on a large four-sheet Technicolor poster, fleeing from unseen enemies, probably struck this pose while sitting astride a beer barrel rigged up as some sort of animated rocking horse. Stars occasionally had stand-ins to do their poster work, and their heads were superimposed later. Posters for *Wild Orchids* (MGM, 1929) showing a bespangled Greta Garbo passionately entwined with a turbaned Nils Asther were actually made from photographs of Asther's stand-in holding Garbo's stand-in. The impression of Garbo's face was taken either from stills of a scene taken on the set or from a gallery session.*

When space was allocated in a studio and the necessary lights and equipment were installed, the gallery was also used for portrait photography. But this practice, begun around 1921 or 1922, did not become firmly established until 1925; and even by 1930 only Paramount, MGM, RKO, and a few other studios had allocated suitable space for galleries.

---

* More recently, when it came time to shoot the poster art for *Some Like It Hot* (1959), the pregnant Marilyn Monroe was not available, and a model stood in for her between Tony Curtis and Jack Lemmon. Monroe's face was later affixed to the body.

Most of the time the photographer used standing stages or undisturbed corners of studio lots. Shortly after Keyes set up his gallery at Famous Players–Lasky, Jack Freulich (see Notes on Other Photographers), head still and portrait photographer at Universal, also got one going.

Initially, it took some convincing to get the stars to give up their favorite private photographers, many of whom had the added allure of photographing the leaders of Los Angeles society and whose work leaned toward their fashionable soft-focus salon style left over from the teens. But since it was the studio who organized the sittings, the stars had little choice—unless they were willing to pay for these sessions themselves.

The studio portrait gallery quickly proved itself to be a boon for the publicity departments, however, which now had the final and most important step toward selling their product—the portraits that were sent out to the magazines. The publicity department's job was not always an enviable one. While it is often said that in Hollywood's heyday there was an audience for any movie that was churned out, with a yearly choice of seven hundred to one thousand new films, some movies were obviously worse than others. With such films, the gallery photographers and stars had their work cut out for them. Each portrait had to attain for the star the effect that on the set had taken a battery of studio lighting, an army of studio technicians, weeks of preparation and of shooting, and a supporting cast—a fact that was not lost on the photographers.

Certainly not all of the stars enjoyed these nonetheless necessary sessions, and still fewer arrived with ideas of their own, as Joan Crawford and Katharine Hepburn did. Often stars would do their best to avoid these sessions or to put them off. Only a very few of the very biggest stars could exercise the right to refuse gallery work if they believed it was not specifically tied to the exploitation of a particular film. There are virtually no modern-dress photographs of Greta Garbo between 1934 (*The Painted Veil*) and 1939 (*Ninotchka*), since she did only period dramas during this time and allowed herself to be photographed only in costumes from these films—something that distanced her even further from her diminishing American public. While other great stars of the thirties may have had the same rights and privileges accorded Garbo by her studio (of course, MGM had no choice with Garbo, since suspension didn't frighten her), it was rare for them to exercise it to the degree that Garbo did, refusing to do any merchandising tie-ins whatsoever.*

And so established stars and neophytes, the camera-happy and the

* In a tie-in arrangement the studio would loan a star's name and face to a cigarette, soap, or other product, and the manufacturer would pay for prime space in national magazines to pro-

camera-shy alike were summoned to the portrait gallery. By the end of the 1920's, the changeover from the private photographer to the studio photographer was complete.

Once an actor was signed, the studio began immediately to create an image. A biography was made, and a session at the portrait gallery was organized. Bud Graybill explained the process:

If the newcomers felt any self-consciousness about posing, it was taken out of them soon after they arrived at the studio. If, say, a man like Bob Taylor arrived, first he would go to William Burns to learn how to talk; then he might be taught how to sing, if there were a chance of that. Taylor went to the gym to build up his shoulders, because he was effeminate in appearance. He was such a beautiful guy when he came to the studio that he looked more like a girl. They worked him in the gym until he came out with broad shoulders; he became a great horseman and was able to make great Westerns. You'd photograph him smoking a pipe, wearing heavy cardigans, doing pictures like *Stand Up and Fight* [1939]—all to make him more masculine in appeal, like Gable. His widow's peak was toned down a bit so it wasn't quite so prominent. It was a business in those days—they were manufacturing a star. We had eighty-five featured players and about thirty-five stars at Metro then. The other studios would do the same. The difference in one studio's visual portrait style from another's would be in the personalities under contract. One thing about MGM, though, was that the idea behind the stars was to make them seem more glamorous, more remote, not so accessible.

The photographers' job was to show the stars as everything the publicity department had made them out to be. The work of the Hollywood photographers had to arouse expectations, suggest promise, capture myths, and crown success. What they did was more complex than mere corrective cosmetics—rather, they traced the emerging mystery of the star's image. For example, in the early portrait of Rita Hayworth, a pretty but still pudgy nineteen-year-old, already her potential is apparent but

James Stewart, 1937. Photographed by Ted Allan. Stewart, fresh from Broadway and new on the MGM lot, has just completed After the Thin Man. *The character that he will be best known for—the folksy, homespun man of the people—has not yet been formulated. Ted Allan recalled: "Two years after Stewart had been with the studio, we still didn't know what the hell to do with him. Was he a comedian, or a romantic leading man? We tried photographing him outside, leaning over fences, working with a shovel, with a tennis racket—but while that worked with Robert Taylor in helping to make him more athletic, it didn't work with Stewart. There was no problem in making him look handsome—he had great eyes and a generous mouth, but in the time I worked with him, I wouldn't have guessed he'd become a star."*

---

mote their product and the new film at least a month before its release. Ever since the impact made by Mary Pickford and the cold cream, it was evident to all concerned that these promotional link-ups were valuable sales outlets for the studios. Not only did Garbo veto any such use of her image, but when, in 1948, she toyed with the idea of making a comeback, there was an additional clause in her contract that stated: "In no event shall we be entitled to use your name and likeness—in connection with so-called 'commercial tie-ups' advertising or publicizing any products, commodities or services without your written consent thereto. We shall not have the right to utilize any of the results and proceeds of your services hereunder in connection with any photoplay other than the photoplay referred to [*La Duchesse de Langaise*] hereof." (One of the best known of all the advertising slogans of the 1930's claimed that "nine out of ten Hollywood stars use Lux." Now we know the one who didn't.)

85

undeveloped. The portrait taken a year later shows us a woman, not only firm of flesh and smooth of skin but mature, mysterious, assured—a woman revealed before she herself has experienced the emotions and events that will shape her character. In one year she has gone from nineteen to thirty-five, from *jeune fille* to *maîtresse femme*, with all the ripeness, beauty, and knowledge that nature would have brought in its own time. But art and ambition had already revealed these qualities to us, and her self-confidence and energy had made us accept them.

It was inevitable that a close professional relationship should arise between the actors and actresses and the men who shot their portraits. The sessions were lightened by music and by banter in an effort to relax

Rita Hayworth, 1939 and 1941. Photographed by A. L. ("Whitey") Schaefer for Columbia. As head of the portrait gallery at Columbia, Schaefer photographed Rita Hayworth for more than five years. When the photograph above was taken, she had appeared in several movies as the girl down the street. The studio realized that Hayworth had the potential to become something dynamic, but they weren't sure if she would be their Ann Sheridan or their Hedy Lamarr. Hayworth had the physical presence of

86

Sheridan—her body's energy and thrust were American—but the facial expression—withdrawn, languid, enigmatic—was European. Both strains are apparent but not yet connected. The photograph above was taken a year and a half later. Rita Hayworth has emerged. She is American vitality combined with European allure. With Hayworth the studio broke through and created for the first time an American exotic—Wedekind's Lulu without the final sting.

the stars so that they could achieve a state in which their physical presence would take on the quality that had brought them to the top and kept them there, even after the initial excitement, based on unfamiliarity, youth, beauty, and talent, had worn away.

What happened in the galleries was an extraordinary thing, something that was beyond the ken of the studios and that owed nothing to contracts, scripts, or the publicity department. To achieve the effect of the great portraits, it was necessary for the sitters to reach a state of trust with the photographer so total that they would unconsciously reveal the very hunger that had driven them to the place where they now found themselves. What was created in those galleries depended as much on the photographer as on the subject, and it took a very special breed of photographer to capture not the idealized self-images the subjects may have had or the roles they played and the masks behind which they hid, but the central emotion that most of us are unable to express because it leaves us so exposed. Rarely did either subject or artist analyze these sittings; it was their work, and they did it.

These portraits have an elusive, haunting beauty that time and fashion cannot fade. Perhaps, as George Hurrell once said, the stars felt themselves to be the children of the gods, and it may be that time has proved them right. In the images produced by the great photographers we see not the faces of mortals like ourselves but the likeness of gods.

When I was sent to Rome by MGM—to take over the shooting of
Ben-Hur [1926]—Irving Thalberg said to me, "Karl, I don't care what
scheme of lighting you use, my stars have to be beautiful." You see, that's
all they were interested in. What they were selling was stars.

—Karl Struss

We can enjoy the sumptuously mounted star vehicles of the thirties today, looking now like documentaries of a vanished world, in the way we might marvel at the achievements of earlier civilizations. We gasp at their profligate wealth. We look at these old films not for the mechanics of the plot but for the excuse they offer us to admire the works of great designers, costumers, photographers, and stars, and for this the close-up is the dramatic highlight. These moments are as gripping to us now as they were when they were first filmed.

In MGM's opulent musical *Dancing Lady* (1933), Joan Crawford plays an ambitious hoofer in a Broadway chorus with "those sort of eyes" for the show's rough-hewn "hands-off" director (Clark Gable). Off-stage the simmering antagonism that mars their working relationship is relaxed in a verbal sparring match that avoids the message their eyes relay. She achieves a truce and wheels around to exit. He raises his hand in a good-natured reflex action that would send her out with a playful pat on the bottom. But before he has a chance to complete his action, she turns around to look at him, catching his hand in midair. The reason for her backward glance is lost in the rush of emotion as the camera moves in for a medium-close shot of the couple from the waist up, showing the barely perceptible movement of his hand in line with the curve of the small of her back. In a pas de deux brilliantly timed and executed, she falls into his embrace, and the camera cuts to an extreme close-up of two radiant profiles. The effect is rapturous.

The close-up—the electric, intimate moment of emotional release that climaxed a movie—was this medium's contribution to art. It remains in the memory long after the film itself has faded and was raised to the level of art in the portrait gallery, where the same effect had to be produced independent of script, scenery, and reels of atmospheric build-up. During the first, floundering years of sound, when cameras were kept to two primitive positions—the long shot and the medium shot—the magical effect of the close-up, almost impossible to achieve with the unwieldy, boxed-in sound camera, was sustained through the work of the portrait photographers. The portraits that came out of this transitional period (1928–30) affected the lighting and filming of the celebrated movie close-ups when the motion picture achieved some camera mobility. Not only did these photographers create their own style in portrait photography, but they defined the image of the Hollywood star and with it the overall look of the movies in the 1930's.

The first step was to move away from the sweet, Victorian portraiture with which society and art photographers had dominated the field in the twenties. Partly because of the slow film, these images were soft, their highlights all aglow and the backgrounds a blur because the cameras' apertures had to be kept wide open. Poor newsprint reproductions further weakened them. The results, while decorative in their own right, contributed little to popular understanding or appreciation of the natures that had so attracted audiences to their screen idols.

From the beginning, the studio portrait photographers tried to convey a direct, person-to-person appeal. But they were intimidated by the established forms of portraiture, which consisted of cropping posed long shots to close-ups. (Later on, as the publicity department gained more and more control in the studios, even this important privilege was taken from them.) Timidly, hesitantly, almost imperceptibly, the studio photographers moved away from the recognized rules of standard portrait photography that had defined society matrons and chorus beauties through recognizable props and poses—the full-length, in-costume studies of celebrated theatrical and operatic stars whom the public recognized because of their roles. While film stars were also photographed with recognizable movie props—sitting on cans of films, leaning against studio stages or arc lights—these were gimmicky, and portraits of the stars in costume from their films were shot specifically to promote just that film. But the recognized standard form of photographing movie stars was the head shot, previously employed only for men of state or of science and letters.

Irene Rich, 1929.
Photographed by Russell Ball.

The apparent shyness of the Hollywood photographers can be attributed in part to the temperamental great stars—Norma Talmadge, Corinne Griffith, Mae Murray, Rudolph Valentino, Gloria Swanson, Douglas Fairbanks, Mary Pickford—who were more likely to dictate than to let themselves be dictated to by the studios and who felt free to go to established independent photographers like Russell Ball and Lansing Brown if the results of the studio photographers failed to please them. The untried, inexperienced studio employees were wary of upsetting their sitters with new techniques of posing.

As long as the studio photographers were not in a position to direct their subjects, they couldn't hope to elicit or present the unique personalities that were projected and adored on the screen. It was not their equipment that was at fault—it remained unchanged for decades—but

Margaret Sullavan, 1933.
Photographed by Jack Freulich.
Freulich founded the portrait gallery
at Universal in 1922 and ran it until
1935, when he was replaced by his
former assistant, Ray Jones.

rather the approach of the photographer, which had to acquire a force-
fulness that would enable them to infuse the dynamism of the cinematic
close-up into the still portrait.

Among the great Hollywood portrait photographers, there was only one
woman, Ruth Harriet Louise. She arrived in Hollywood when the technique of portraiture was developing into an increasingly personal collaboration between the photographer and the subject, a technique that relied on
the gentle, persuasive talents of the photographer. The body of her work
at MGM (April 1925 to March 1930) illustrates the transition from the
stiff, formal, and distant nineteenth-century style of portrait photography
to the free-spirited, almost explosive portraits of the 1930's.

Louise was only nineteen when, on a visit to Hollywood with her director brother Mark Sandrich, she signed her first contract with the newly formed MGM and became the studio's official portrait photographer. Her innovation lay more in the way in which she approached her subjects than in technique. For her the joy of photography consisted in getting to the soul of her sitter by avoiding the artificiality that comes from "sitting" for portraits. To prevent the stars from merely repeating the poses they were used to and to help put them at their ease, she would create an easy informality in her gallery, finding out beforehand their tastes in music and the subjects that interested them. The stars loved her work and even left the final decision of which photos to print and which to destroy up to her—a fact that did not endear her to the publicity department, which didn't like their employees to become too independent.

Louise's portraits resulted from her thoughtful cropping of full-length shots. It is necessary to bear this in mind when looking at her work (as well as the work of most of the photographers of that period). The finished portrait was often actually only one-seventh of the original shot, enlarged to fill the space formerly occupied by the full-length pose. Her negatives—of which she was given complete control—required extremely careful handling, since the slightest scratch on the minute face of the original would be magnified when it was blown up to create the final print. Al St. Hilaire, who worked for Louise, described her retoucher as "almost a master miniaturist": "The image of the portraits was so delicate in the last stages, the lines so softened, the shadowing so muted, that it was very difficult to retouch them without it showing. But the man she had working for her was incredible. Even when you blew the print up you could hardly tell what he'd done—and he'd done a lot."

There is about Louise's work a delicacy, a shy, appealing privacy, that established an immediate bond with the viewer. She maintained a distance that allowed people to feel secure and captured a quality of innocence and vulnerability in her subjects which had originally drawn us to them but which we began to see in the Hollywood portraits only when Louise revealed it to us. Her Garbo is a girl fresh from her homeland, still awkward and tentative with eyes wide and curious, exposed and aware that she is being observed, and poised for instant flight should safe boundaries be crossed and confidences violated.

What worked with the most elusive of all the stars worked also with the self-infatuated Mae Murray, the effervescent Marion Davies, the romantic John Gilbert, and the spiritual Lillian Gish, with the established stars as well as the awed newcomers, like fifteen-year-old Nina Mae McKinney, the black star of King Vidor's *Hallelujah!* (1929). Louise was

Greta Garbo, 1926. Photographed by Ruth Harriet Louise for MGM. Louise was the only woman ever to be employed as a photographer by a major Hollywood studio. In 1925, when she was twenty-two years old, she was given her own portrait gallery at MGM. Her technique was of her day, but she conveyed something new —something that no one else had caught—about the essence of stardom: "Garbo is hard to photograph," Louise once explained. "She has so many sides to her personality that one cannot do her justice easily in one picture. She is so young and sad; she has so many moods, and even when she smiles I always sense a great sadness."

clearly in the vanguard of the photographers who would revolutionize Hollywood portrait photography. Her portraits of Garbo over the space of a few years trace the actress's emergence into her flawless self in images that command with one look and appear to fade with the next, whispering invitations even as she recedes into the white matte paper that contains her.

These lyrical studies reveal Louise's exploration of the star mystique. Yet at the very brink of achieving that final collaboration between artist and subject, and thus giving the still photograph the vitality of the cinematic close-up, she halts, unable or unwilling to step across the line that divides the passive from the active. Louise's failure to cross the Rubicon that separated her from the sitter was a question not of logic but of instinct. It was in her nature to be empathic. But to create dynamic portraits that captured the energy of the soul and made of it something in-

comparable to see, the photographer had to be the active agent, regardless of the sitter's attitude or sex.

By the time Louise left MGM, her work seems to have reached a curious impasse: she had expanded her technique to its limits, but no eye, however sharp or brilliantly attuned to the special quality of the subject, and no technique, however painstakingly or lovingly executed, can compensate for the distance between photographer and sitter. Trapped behind the camera, at the distance prescribed by the formal long shot, the portrait photographer was an isolated agent in the process of divining the sitter's innermost self, and only a sensitivity such as Louise's could compensate for this. Ruth Harriet Louise's work testifies to her place as one of the truly important Hollywood portrait photographers, but it was another photographer who exploded out of the old form of Hollywood portraiture.

George Hurrell, like Louise, had already established a reputation as a photographer outside the movie industry. It was his photographs of members of Los Angeles society that brought him to the attention of the romantic Latin star Ramon Novarro, who came to him in 1929 for photographs that would present a more forceful, masculine side to his boyishly winning personality. The Mexican actor was so pleased with the results that he showed them to other actors and actresses, including his co-star in *The Student Prince*, Norma Shearer, who was also trying to change her image.

Hurrell's first session with a movie star had been informal. The Shearer session was a royal visit. She arrived at his little studio on Lafayette Park Place on a Saturday afternoon in a yellow Rolls-Royce with a complete wardrobe and an entourage that included her hairdresser and a makeup man. "They weren't making her look sexy enough at the studio," recalled Hurrell, "and the idea was to get her looking real wicked and siren-like, which wasn't the image she had at the time, and so I suppose nobody thought she could get away with it."

That day's work revealed a new Shearer. Her sleek black hair was made to look bushy and fell across her forehead suggestively. A brocaded silken robe was allowed to slip over one shoulder and reveal a leg. Shadows curved and elongated, suggesting more than was actually there. The results dramatically affected both Shearer's and Hurrell's careers and contributed a new word to the movie-goer's vernacular—*glamour*.

Although at this period Hurrell still worked with the diffusing Vertone lenses, he "stopped" them down as much as possible to achieve a

Johnny Weissmuller, 1934, Tarzan and His Mate. *Photographed by George Hurrell. "There were no two stars alike in beauty, but each one had a special quality that was considered beautiful. They were all photogenic, or else they never would have made it. My primary effort, with any type of camera, is to capture that fleeting expression and try to get that spontaneous look in the eyes, a kind of momentary feeling— something that vanishes in a second. On the movie screen the length of the scene and the action produces the expression with no problem. The actor merely turns on an expression until the director says cut."*

more sharply defined image and used shadows to emphasize character and establish a mood. He moved his camera so close to his sitter that there was little room left on the negative for anything other than the face and what lay behind it. He rejected the traditional brightly lit, diffused style of photography with its amorphous sentimentality.

For Hurrell, glamour meant sexy pictures. His photographs made the stars willing participants, eager to visit his galleries and trusting themselves to his volatile genius to an exceptional degree. Loretta Young, waxing enthusiastic about her sessions with Hurrell, put her finger on it: "What I liked about the way Hurrell photographed us was that he made you look so *glamorous.* Your skin looked so shiny—as if you could reach out and touch it. I know the secret with him—he was the first man who said he didn't want any makeup. You used to put a little oil on your face, and that was about all."

The original, unretouched negatives of photographers like Hurrell, Ted Allan, Bob Coburn, Ernest Bachrach, and Whitey Schaefer reveal how confident the great beauties and heroes of that period had to be when they sat for their portraits. There was no grease paint or pancake makeup to hide the freckles, wrinkles, or facial hair that made some of the glamorous leading ladies look more like little boys; the pores around the eyebrows, plucked stylishly thin, are magnified into small craters; lips known the world over for their full, seductive shapes are often less than perfect and surprisingly hard. Their hair would be immaculately done up, and so would their wardrobe, producing an even more incongruous effect with their bare faces and necks wrinkled from the contortions of posing. But these negatives do not disillusion. Here are certainly very beautiful human beings, but they offer in addition a testament to the degree of collaboration that existed and that made these stars willing to reveal face and form in their naked, unadorned states, offering the photographer a rare canvas on which he could proceed to paint with his lights.

Of course, the stars had final approval of the prints, and they relied on the photographer (and the retoucher) to remove any visible defects. From the instant the star stepped into the gallery, the photographer took into consideration the work to be done later in the darkroom, and by the army of expert retouchers on the negative, at which time any mistakes in posing or lighting could be corrected. Using a fine point on a special pencil, the retouchers lightened spots and wrinkles with infinitesimal additions of lead. Darkening an area on a negative was done by carefully scraping the emulsion from the dark areas with a knife. They cleaned dirty teeth, replaced missing ones, and straightened crooked ones; they cleared the eyes if they were dull or bloodshot; they lengthened necks

Jean Harlow, 1933, Bombshell *(MGM). Photographed by George Hurrell, using an 8 × 10 view camera on a tripod with an 18-inch lens; exposure: one-half second at f16. "I used a 1000-watt spot above and behind Harlow's head plus a 1000-watt floodlight from the camera as a fill light. The spot was to the right of the camera and about five feet above Harlow. I always lit Harlow's face with a single spot because the definite shadows emphasized her strong features: her deep-set eyes made it necessary for her to tilt her head down. Her high forehead and short chin were a serious consideration in lighting her, but the cleft in her chin was an asset because it helped balance her forehead."*

and eyelashes, whittled waists, and excised ungainly pounds. A precise art, retouching also required very precise instructions on each negative so that the stars wouldn't all come out looking alike. There are pictures of W. C. Fields that make him seem as wholesome as Baby LeRoy, and a number of photos of Mae West in which her celebrated curves have been flattened to the point where her jewelry seems suspended near her neck and wrists. And since retouchers were paid by the hour, it was in their interest to do as much as possible. The less precise the instructions, the more likely it was that the face would take on that lifeless, enameled look so favored by the Japanese. The retouchers were artists in their own right, and the photographers were the first to give them their share of the credit, but no delicate retouching of the negative or beautiful printing could turn

Cary Grant, 1936.
Photographed by Ted Allan.

an ordinary portrait into a work of art if there had been no inspiration in the mind of the man behind the camera.

Hurrell had trained at the Chicago School of Fine Arts to become a painter, beginning his studies at the precise moment when the art world was in turmoil and the old rules regarding landscapes and portraiture were undergoing ruthless re-examination. By reducing things to their geometric elements, painters like Picasso and Braque sought to express the inner characters of objects by probing behind the outer descriptions of form, making their work crackle with the vigor of a direct and furious exploration of their subjects. But while this stimulated the art world, it alienated the public, who were not ready to respond to this vision of the world.

Hurrell's approach was influenced by this new movement in painting, though his powerfully romantic style came from an older tradition in art. He was enthusiastically promoted by MGM's publicity department, and his success encouraged photographers at the other studios, directly and indirectly.*

In 1928 the Danish film director Carl Dreyer shook the artistic world. While everybody else was furiously converting to sound, he produced a silent masterpiece, *Le Passion de Jeanne d'Arc*. But his audacity lay not so much in the film's silence as in its use of extreme close-ups, especially of the French actress Falconetti. The film concentrated on Joan's trial and burning, and this technique enabled the director to extract the ultimate in fervor, terror, anguish, and spirituality from his actress and to communicate to his audience the intense and conflicting emotions Joan must have felt before her inquisitors at Rouen and later at the stake. We know from Falconetti how emotionally and physically draining it was for her to work with Dreyer. She never made another film, but the critics felt Falconetti's personal discomfiture was a small price to pay for art, and they were in ecstasy.

The Hollywood portrait photographers, using this same technique, achieved results as hypnotic and splendid; yet they received no such critical recognition. But their portrait sessions, with the stars fixed by the relentless lens like butterflies on a lepidopterist's pin for their perfection to be captured forever, had their own unforeseen side effects.

* When Frank Powolny approached Loretta Young to let him take her portraits, she took an afternoon off to pose for him after showing him some of Hurrell's work and telling him, "Just take a look at those Hurrell things. That's what I want to look like."

On the whole, these sessions were characterized by a fairly easy working relationship between two professionals who shared the same goal —to create photographs that would stimulate the public to spend money to see a film. Generally the mood was kept as informal as possible; but for some photographers, in William Walling's words, "It was important to try and keep a professional distance, or else you'd go crazy." These sittings were occasionally relieved with laughter. Bob Coburn, who photographed Merle Oberon for more than ten years, said, "It's hard to explain how you get people to do things, to respond. You work with them a lot. Sometimes they become your second nature. I'd be talking and telling them things and be focused, ready to shoot, so that when I got what I wanted I'd shoot like a madman. I just shot, shot, shot with those huge 8 × 10's. Some photographers would horse around and take three shots in the time I'd have taken three hundred. I'm exaggerating, but you had to shoot a lot to get that photograph of a Hayworth or an Oberon that would make everybody get excited when they saw it."

For the less secure stars, the challenge of having to define and revitalize themselves continuously before the still camera while still retaining the immediacy of their first exposure inevitably produced moments of emotional crisis and self-doubt. Some of them, like Carole Lombard and Joan Crawford, thought nothing of spending an hour or more getting emotionally prepared between changes, and they retained this excitement in front of the cameras throughout their careers. Others began to reveal the doubts and insecurities that lay behind their success. Loretta Young pointed out the psychological difference between these sessions and working on a set: "In motion pictures you were trained never to look into the camera. In the gallery you had to start doing something that was against all the rules. It's not easy in any case to come into a room, close the door, walk to the camera, and say 'Hello' without looking stiff or silly or unnatural when you're supposed to be *you*. I knew what I was when I was playing a part, but I didn't know *me*. And I never really knew how to behave like myself if there was a camera around. The only way I got around that was by trying to pretend that the camera was somebody instead of just a black hole."

Some stars had to have a drink (Errol Flynn, Jean Harlow), some had to be practically dragged to the gallery (Veronica Lake, John Barrymore), some created problems once they got there (Miriam Hopkins, Constance Bennett, Joan Fontaine, Charles Laughton), and some would rather have been taken off salary than report to the gallery for the obligatory seasonal "drape art," or pin-ups (Loretta Young). Others, however, resorted to various degrees of exhibitionism once they got there. Some

Madeleine Carroll, 1937. Photographed by Ted Allan for Selznick International. "Because the 8 × 10 negative was so necessary to the inexpensive mass printing needed by the studios, there was no such thing as custom enlargements or recomposing. It was essential to compose directly onto the negative. The weightless camera and the ball-and-socket head (built especially for me by the MGM engineering department) allowed me to view the posing, lighting, and composition on the ground glass as I moved and adjusted the camera to suit the subject. To create dimension, it

was necessary to control the planes of illumination. The conventional method then was to shoot with a high-key single-source floodlight or soft skylight illumination. The MGM studio engineering department built a set of portable boom lights for me. I used them for back and side line-lights and found it helpful to swing a free-wheeling boom light across a face to find the most interesting angle of light for the subject. In my portraits I have a small area of pure white that allows the skin tones to be printed darker and with definition."

women would arrive in the gallery, shed their robe, and lie completely unself-consciously before the camera (Maria Montez, Marilyn Monroe, Jean Harlow). They knew that the photographer couldn't show them that way; their objective was not to seduce but to inspire the artist to take great photographs.

Ted Allan described his first official session with Jean Harlow after she had approved him as her portrait photographer, which coincided with the studio-engineered change of her free-spirited and sexy image to a more demure "brownette" look, which it was hoped would win over more of the women in the audience:

Of all the people I thought wouldn't feel self-conscious when posing—after all, the whole basis of her personality on the screen was outgoing and freewheeling —it was Jean. Yet when it was time for the stills, she was—terribly. When she

(Left) Jean Harlow, 1935. Photographed by Ted Allan. "When I first auditioned for the job of replacing Hurrell as exclusive photographer for Jean Harlow—Russell Ball and Tom Evans were also trying out—the first requisite was that I present her as more of a lady. I insisted that her hair be toned down into what Jack Dawn [head of MGM's makeup and hairdressing department] termed brownette."

Jean Harlow with Franchot Tone, 1936, Suzy (MGM). Photographed by Ted Allan. This picture was taken a year before Harlow's death. Gone is the extravagant, overemphatic sexuality and the clumsy brownette shopgirl look. What we see now is her warmth, her friendliness, her sincerity. And surprisingly, she is much prettier than one would have imagined. Harlow is blossoming into the woman the hero would have wanted at home, rather than the girl he kept on the side.

arrived I already had everything set up in the four corners of the room, so that I could go zing-zing-zing, because she'd change so fast. While she did that, I'd change the four spots and set up a new series. It was very rapid, and she loved that. One of these photographs was a sort of "end of the pier" scene, with fishnets hanging down. She went over and threw a fishnet over her shoulders and then suggested that it would show up better if there were bare skin beneath it, since the net was the same color as the knit suit she was wearing. I went back to the camera to adjust things, and when I looked up she was walking around with this thing wrapped around her and nothing underneath. I thought, "Wow," and tried to stand between her and her hairdresser, who might come in the door any minute. But it didn't bother her at all. It was more as if she were playing a part, calculated to get me on her side. She figured that if I were

turned on, I'd take better pictures. And she'd go on during a sitting as long as I would. Her limousine would be out there waiting all day. After she'd had a couple of drinks, she'd get into the mood and begin to enjoy posing. Then she'd go like wildfire. I realized then that she always needed something personal—that feeling of being liked. It made her feel secure.

The stars may have used different ploys to help get them through the sessions, but the underlying motivation was the same: fear. Although in 1930 the industry was in its infancy, there were already too many corners haunted by former screen idols like Mae Murray, one of the legendary stars of the twenties. Virtually overnight the public had turned from her, and by 1930 she was forgotten. Her attempted comebacks were mocked by the same journalists who had earlier fought to interview her.

But if a film failed, stars could always reassure themselves by shifting the responsibility to the story, their co-star, or the director. In the gallery, they were alone. Laszlo Willinger explained the reason for this fear: "Suddenly you see the private person. People become actors for the purpose of *not* showing their private selves, and when they don't have a role to hide behind, it's always a problem. Especially for a pretty woman. Men don't care as much; anyway, they don't dare admit it. But women are more aware of age and of the younger girls coming up behind them."

Loretta Young has spent most of her life in front of the camera. She made her film debut at the age of five, was a leading lady by thirteen, and became a star before she had reached twenty-one. She once described her fifty-year-long film career as "a love affair with the camera," but then added, "I'd rather do two films back to back than spend an hour in the portrait gallery. It was very hard work, because you were acting all the time and your concentration was intense, yet you felt you were being dissected. The person behind that camera is looking at you constantly. If he doesn't like you, or if you don't like him, it's very difficult to work. You have to be able to relax, and you can't do that when you're embarrassed—you know that the lens magnifies everything."

Irene Dunne prefers not to discuss her sessions with RKO's brilliant Ernest Bachrach. She remembers him respectfully but considers the more than fifteen years she worked with him to be an unimportant part of her career. She had never enjoyed these sessions, she explained, and couldn't see why, after all these years, she should waste time talking about this side of her work.

At the other extreme is Katharine Hepburn, Bachrach's favorite subject. She loved their sessions and loved being photographed—even

Robert Taylor, 1936.
Photographed by Ted Allan for MGM.

107

though it meant getting up at four or five o'clock in the morning in order to be dressed and ready in the gallery by nine, just as one would for a film. "There's a very good reason for it," Hepburn explained. "Sheer vanity. Joan Crawford also took her photo sessions seriously, because she took a very good picture. I photographed better than I looked, so it was easy for me. . . . I let myself go before the camera. I mean, you can't photograph a dead cat. You have to offer something. Once you get in front of the camera, it's not how you look that's important but how you come across. And if you're thinking of how you look, you'll be in a bad way."

Norma Shearer, similar in type to Irene Dunne, nevertheless felt secure and happy working with George Hurrell and loved their sessions together—and this despite the potential disadvantage of having a strabismus—a cast in her eyes—that made it difficult for her to look directly into the camera without looking cross-eyed. Because of this, she was as particular about her portrait photographers as she was about her cameraman. Ted Allan recalled the time he photographed her, in 1935, when she was playing Juliet to Leslie Howard's Romeo. "I was concerned about Miss Shearer's very close-set eyes. An improvised gallery was set up in the center of a bare stage. The circumstance, with its lack of intimacy, was as cold as the famous star's attitude. Miss Shearer had arranged for a large full-length mirror in front of which she would pose. If she was viewing her best angle in the mirror, I certainly wasn't getting it in my camera, which was several feet to the side. She was concentrating on her mirrored image, and I made the mistake of saying, 'I'm over here, Miss Shearer.' The sitting ground to a halt. During lunch I audaciously scraped an area of silver off the mirror and finished the sitting shooting through the mirror. After that I never heard from her again."

Obviously, a good rapport between the subject and the artist was vital—Hepburn with Bachrach, Garbo with Bull, Oberon and later Hayworth with Coburn, Crawford and Shearer with Hurrell and later with Willinger. Hurrell agreed: "If I didn't get a lively reaction out of the person, I didn't get much out of it myself." When it clicked, something more than just good photographs resulted: that third thing—the image—emerged.

Katharine Hepburn, looking at a floor covered with her portraits, concurred, and added, "It wasn't arrived at self-consciously. I was just a kid when I began posing for Ernie Bachrach. He was beginning to feel his oats, and so was I. We both had something to gain in our work. Now that girl there," she said laughing, pointing to a photograph of herself in a large hat, "liked to show off. I can't think of any other explanation. She saw herself in many different moods, and she was rather interested

Loretta Young, 1938, Suez *(Fox). Photographed by Frank Powolny. Powolny was born in Vienna, where he was taught to use a camera while still a child by his father, a photographer at the Imperial Court. When he was thirteen Powolny came to America and began work as a stonemason in Nebraska. He quit a few years later and went to Los Angeles, where he was hired as an assistant cinematographer to the famous cameraman Jules Cronjager. Powolny's reputation as one of the finest of the early still photographers was established after he worked with directors John Ford (*The Iron Horse, 1924*), Frank Borzage (*Seventh Heaven, 1927*), and F. W. Murnau (*Sunrise, 1927; Four Devils, 1928; City Girl, 1930*). His reputation as a portrait photographer was established by his five-year collaboration with Loretta Young.*

in what was going on. Now if Bachrach got somebody like that, who enjoyed standing around doing those crazy things, loving to pose, naturally he would like her. We were compatible. Ernie was just easy to work for. He didn't make you feel self-conscious."

Ernest Bachrach never ceased to study his craft, to observe what others were doing, and to keep trying for new effects in his work that would illuminate his subjects. He wrote about some of the problems inherent in his craft in a 1932 article in *American Cinematographer*:

It is a common misconception that screen stars are inevitably easy subjects for the portrait photographer. Not by any means. . . . They often become painfully self-conscious and camera shy in the portrait gallery. Of course, on the

Irene Dunne, 1933.
Photographed by Ernest Bachrach.
"Actors and actresses only too often want to appear not as they actually are but as they think they are. Almost all comedians prefer to look tragic. The women frequently want to be made to look like Garbo or Ann Harding or Dolores Del Rio, according to their type. It takes diplomacy of the highest order to secure fifty or a hundred different poses in the space of a half-hour or so while at the same time getting some that will suit the vanity of the sitter."

Katharine Hepburn, 1935.
Photographed by Ernest Bachrach.
Bachrach photographed Hepburn
from 1932, when she came to RKO,
until 1939, when her contract expired
and she left Hollywood to appear on
Broadway. "He liked to photograph
me, and I liked to pose for him. We
were compatible."

set the star is completely immersed in his creative work so that there is literally no consciousness of the fact that he is being photographed; his mind is completely absorbed by his characterization, direction, and so on. In the portrait gallery, on the other hand, he has nothing to think about except that he is being photographed.

George Hurrell, whose success with most of Hollywood's glamorous stars—even the notoriously difficult ones—made him a legend, was the only portrait photographer besides Clarence S. Bull to have a session with Garbo at MGM after 1930. It was set up to publicize her second talking picture, *Romance* (1930), when Hurrell was the hot new photographer at the studio. Although he achieved some superb results, their meeting was not a personal success. Garbo climbed the three flights to his gallery (the one that only a few months before had been Ruth Harriet Louise's). The problem, according to Hurrell, was really a matter of style:

I always liked to work with people who would put themselves in my hands somewhat. I don't mean that I would have complete freedom all the time, but at least to the point where they would be more resilient. Garbo was pretty much self-styled. She was probably the sexiest gal among the whole bunch of them, but that wasn't what she was selling. There was a stiffness about her. It didn't help that I was the wild, hollering kind, leaping all over the place, talking, slamming on records that I thought might get her going. She was amused, I think, but she clammed up.

Yet before the afternoon sun had gone, after they had gotten the fashion and poster art out of the way, Hurrell produced some of the most tender portraits ever taken of the already legendary and increasingly remote star. He explained:

I didn't follow my usual technique with those pictures. For one thing, I didn't want to fool around with setting up lights. That sort of thing had already been done with her on the set; though if I had known that we wouldn't be working together again, I would have gone after portraits with my lighting style. But at the time I was trying to think of a new approach for her. I had a skylight in the roof, and I thought, well, why not use that? I tried going a little dark, with just a little light flooding in from the side if necessary, doing the kinds of things with natural lighting that artists like Vermeer did with paint. The results didn't look as theatrical, and they didn't turn out as dramatic as my usual work; but considering those heavy velvet costumes and that silly hat she wore, I think it served its purpose of promoting her and the film.

Although the close-up portraits are marred by the Empress Eugénie hat and a hairstyle that breaks the classic line of Garbo's brow with girlish curls, Hurrell nevertheless succeeded, partly because of the distance between them and partly because of the natural, soft style of lighting he used to achieve a profoundly moving silence that stands in lyrical contrast to the severe, enigmatic face.

But this was the exception. Generally when there was no rapport between a star and a photographer, the pictures suffered. This is what happened when Garbo's replacement at the studio, Greer Garson, worked with the talented young Eric Carpenter. He had already shot many portraits of Lana Turner, and with great success. But Turner was young and secure, and she was able to accept a man's appreciation without be-

Greta Garbo, 1930, Romance (MGM). Photographed by George Hurrell; costume by Adrian. This was the only time Hurrell photographed Garbo.

coming inhibited. Greer Garson was more reserved, and to evoke her cool, ladylike image she needed a less aggressive personality. Virgil Apger (see Notes on Other Photographers), a very talented still man, was transferred to the gallery to take Garson's portraits.

Ray Jones, whose photographs of Danielle Darrieux for *The Rage of Paris* (1938) were a vital part of the publicity campaign introducing the French star to the American public, discussed the importance of establishing a rapport with his subject in an article in *International Photographer*:

Each time that I focus the camera I find a new problem. . . . The portrait photographer is not only required to produce the vivid coloring, the sparkling eyes and the infinite grace of the majority of these subjects as it might appear on the screen, but must also strive to bring out the spirit and personality that are hidden beneath the lovely mask of flesh. Each and every screen star requires a different kind of treatment. The first problem is to dissect their personality and win their confidence. They must have a feeling of repose when they face the camera, must feel certain you will not depict them in a background that is not in keeping with their personality. Real photography bares the ego of the subject, and you must first determine what this ego really consists of before you can present it.

Loretta Young agreed. "It's a duet between you and him. He has to know you. You don't particularly have to know him, but he has to know you. And to like you." Sometimes, as Hurrell said, "it would get to the point where you were almost making love to the girl. Your camera was so close, you were almost on top of her." Katharine Hepburn put it this way: "You have to think. You have to enjoy. You have to tick. You have to be alive."

A good deal of a photographer's success, then, depended, in Ted Allan's words, on "getting them to relax and enjoy themselves. They could cross you up completely by being stilted and uncomfortable." A few years ago, George Hurrell was commissioned by *New West* magazine to photograph a group of so-called instant celebrities in his thirties style, including John and Maureen Dean, Bianca Jagger, and muscle king Arnold Schwarzenegger. He found the assignment not very interesting since the sitters were unable to give him anything but poses of themselves. An exception was Liza Minnelli, one of the few who understood what was needed and who came prepared to work. Even so, "it wasn't like photographing Crawford," Hurrell explained. "She loved to pose. She gave so much to the still camera—all I had to do was to compose the shot, and she'd be off. She really loved all that dramatic stuff—standing there, very intense. We would spend the whole day working. She would change into twenty different gowns, with hairdos, makeup—everything. No complaints, and lots of enthusiasm."

He continued: "You can create glamour, but the person has to have something—some quality—a drive or an intensity that lights up in front of the camera, or else it won't work. They have to have it physically, but they have to think it too. Just the physical quality alone won't work. There has to be that combination."

For many years after Hurrell left MGM, Joan Crawford insisted he be brought back to photograph her, until the studio hired Laszlo Willinger (who was initially designated Norma Shearer's photographer). Willinger remembered Crawford as "a woman who worked with the photographer rather than telling him, 'show me what you can do.'" This is why Crawford's portraits, especially those taken in the thirties, when she was at the peak of her beauty, are so extravagantly successful. She reveled in her glory, and the portraits that resulted may be the finest testament to her ambition and her triumph.

While the photographers could not afford to show favoritism and had to take the stars as they were sent to them by the publicity department, the stars could prove very particular about who photographed them. They expected the photographer to be available when they were, and if their photographer was busy and they were sent to another, or if they didn't get the treatment they expected, problems would result.

Miriam Hopkins was, like Constance Bennett, a sophisticated blonde, notorious for her sharp tongue and her aversion to sitting for the obligatory portraits. William Walling photographed her for the first time in 1932, when he was in his own gallery at Paramount:

She was being difficult from the moment she arrived, because Richee, who normally photographed her, was elsewhere. Usually she got the full treatment —lounges, cigarettes, satins, the works. But I had been given specific orders to shoot white backgrounds for newspaper cuts, so I put her up against white drops. She said, "What's all this about!" I brought a chaise lounge in. Then she said to me, "Now we're going to have an understanding. My hair is blonde and I want it to look blonde." I took a baby spot—which is a silly lighting anyway— and put it in back of her hair. Then she said, "On second thought, I'd rather be on this side." Here was the spotlight, tight in the camera. I took the slide out, put it in the holder, ran back to the camera, moved the light a little bit to the left, ran back, focused the camera, got the plate holder, pulled the slide out, grabbed the bulb to squeeze it—and she moved again. She did it at least four times. I told her that she was deliberately creating a situation, and I walked out and told Publicity that they weren't paying me to take this kind of abuse.

This kind of behavior on the part of a star could take on frightening proportions. Willinger recalled: "The night before Christmas, after the studio party, I went home. I got a call saying Jeanette MacDonald wants you. That was enough. You weren't asked. You were told. I went back to the studio. A complete camera crew was assembled on one side of the stage. We were there for a couple of hours doing tests—on her eyelashes. I never found out if she used the new ones—each eyelash was glued to her lids separately. The absurdity of it—any time—but on Christmas Eve!"

The problems could get even more ludicrous when it required photographing two or more stars together. This was the case on another of Willinger's assignments, *The Women* (MGM, 1939), whose illustrious all-female cast of stars was headed by the studio's arch rivals, Shearer and Crawford. Both had been at the top for a long time but were seeing their positions threatened, not only by each other but by a whole new crop of starlets coming up from behind, some of whom were also in the film. It was expected that there might be problems at some point, and they surfaced in Willinger's gallery. Both stars wanted him to do their portraits, and both had the right to reject photos they didn't like. In shots of the two of them together, countless prints were rejected. Willinger described what it was like:

Shearer would look at the prints first and say, "Gee, this is a beautiful picture of me, but I really don't like the way Joan Crawford looks." And then Joan would have her turn, and we'd have the same thing. It's a wonder any pictures of them were released at all.

There were two on that film who were easy to work with—Paulette Goddard, because she was ambitious, and Rosalind Russell, because she didn't give a damn. As a result Goddard got practically 90 percent of the stuff that was published, because she made herself available.

One day the three principals took off from filming, just so we could shoot stills. The call was for ten a.m. I'm up there, ready—nobody. It's ten-thirty, eleven—still nobody. Finally Rosalind Russell turns up and says, "Sorry I'm late." I told her, "You're not late. You're the first one here." I walked outside the stage that had been set up for the session. A crew of ten was standing around waiting, including a flower man in case one of them wanted a flower. (I couldn't give them the flower, because that would have been against union rules, and everybody would have walked off.) Finally I saw Norma Shearer's car drive by. It slowed down. She looked out and continued driving around the block. A little behind her was Joan Crawford, who also slowed down, looked out, and drove on. I thought "What the hell's going on here?" I called [publicity director Howard] Strickling and told him, "There are two stars outside driving around the stage and not coming in." He said, "Don't you know what they're doing? Shearer isn't going to come in before Crawford, and Crawford isn't going to come in before Shearer. The only thing I can do is to stand in the middle of the street and stop them." Which he did.

Spencer Tracy, James Cagney, Gary Cooper, Clark Gable, and Humphrey Bogart considered sitting for portraits to be "sissy stuff" and complained more about that than about the hours spent actually working. Tracy, another of Willinger's subjects, hated the obligatory sittings: "He would cut a session down to ten minutes—moved his head from right to left and said goodbye. He was a little less abrupt when Miss Hepburn was there." David Niven used to make Bob Coburn feel like a dentist with an awkward child, "he was so afraid of revealing himself."

William Walling had his hands full with the tricks of a Charles Laughton or a John Barrymore, not to mention the turmoil that ensued when photographing W. C. Fields (with and without Baby LeRoy). It took all of Walling's resourcefulness to cope with these outsize personalities. He explained:

These men could really drive you crazy, because they had that wonderful capacity of putting the photographer on the defensive. This is no way to work, because you're immediately handcuffed. By the time Barrymore came into the gallery he might already have had more than a few nips and most likely would rather have been doing something else.

Jan Kiepura, a European opera singer Paramount thought they could make into a star, arrived in the gallery and insisted that a mirror be placed next to him so that he could look at himself standing there and pulling big dramatic poses. Finally he said to me (and at first I thought he was kidding, because you never quite knew how to take these people), "It is impossible to photograph me, because I have so much personality that it can never come across in a photograph."

Now Cooper was something else—next to Bing Crosby he was the laziest guy who ever walked the face of the earth. Coop would come in, languid all over the place, a stringbean of a man with an easy smile and a great deal of charm. You knew that whatever mood you caught him in, deep down inside he was just thinking of shooting a lion or something. But he'd light a cigarette in that slow way of his while looking straight into the camera, and his fans would see his picture and think they'd bagged a lion. This was a natural ability.

John Engstead, who supervised Cooper's sessions when they were both at Paramount and photographed him a great deal in later years, had

Dorothy Lamour, 1937. Photographed by William Walling, Jr. Lamour is twenty-two years old here. Her first movie, The Jungle Princess (1936), had made her a star—but confined her to a type: the illiterate, good-hearted child of the forest whose missionary parents have been killed by the time we meet her, and she has been lovingly raised by wild animals. Subsequent attempts were made by the studio to transform her into a glamorous leading lady, but the public preferred the sweet, open girl of the jungle.

Charles Laughton, 1932. Photographed by William Walling, Jr. Laughton was chubby and plain, and self-conscious about his lack of good looks. Notoriously difficult on the set, he was, as Walling recalled, even more ill-at-ease in the portrait gallery. But here Walling has produced an image in which sensitivity, soulfulness, and elegance of feeling emerge as other aspects of glamour.

this revealing insight: "Cooper knew more about how to be photographed than any other man I know. The way he handled his face and his six-foot three-inch frame led me to surmise that he must have done considerable homework. . . . He moved with the grace of a panther. I don't think he either liked or disliked photographic sessions, but he endured them because he realized that they were part of his business. . . . One thing that made it easy for Cooper to make stills was his appreciation that cameras photograph the mind. . . . Cooper carried this professionalism to the care of his body, which he kept in top physical condition until his last illness."

There were other male stars, though, who took this aspect of their career quite seriously and were as fussy about their appearance as the women. James Cagney discreetly accentuated his eyebrows and eyes with

makeup to focus attention on his piercing glance, while Errol Flynn applied a virile tan from a jar.

But the stars had to be concerned about their looks, "Yourself— that's the only thing an actor sells," explained Loretta Young,

and that self is not just acting, but looks. There's a perfect example— Montgomery Clift. Before his face was all destroyed in an accident, he was considered one of the most marvelous actors, one of the greats, because his face was so gorgeous and he made everything he did so romantic. If you looked at him, you just died. Then he had the accident. He was the same actor—better, even—saying dialogue exactly the same, but you just thought, "What's he doing?" It's not just acting. It's a combination of what you present to an audience or the cameraman of your looks and your attitude and the words and everything about you. You're selling yourself. And we knew it. Part of making a star was still pictures. There were a lot of people who were stars only because of their still pictures—their movies never meant anything.

Most actresses—at least in my day—we all thought we were gorgeous, because by the time they finished with you, you *were* gorgeous. I heard Bette Davis in an interview one time say that she never could stand her face. And I thought, gosh, she was the most beautiful thing I ever saw in *Jezebel* and *Dark Victory* and *The Letter*. And then she said, "However, when I see my movies today, I was gorgeous!" And she was. She was. At those sessions with the still photographer you could almost tell by their pleasure: "Oh, I love it, it's marvelous, it's great. Just hold that." It wasn't done in the way you saw it in *Blow-Up*. There wasn't an iota of embarrassment or suggestiveness or lewdness or sex. That would have turned us—turned me, anyway—off. It was pure romanticism and what I thought was beauty. They just thought that I was too good to be true, and they would hardly touch me because I might break. That's the feeling I remember most.

Bob Coburn, thinking back to his sessions with Merle Oberon, said, "I'd call her in between pictures, and we'd dream something up, or sometimes we'd just say, 'Let's take some photographs.' Then we'd take anything from a day here and there to three days at the end of a picture. She'd sit there with very little makeup on, and I'd start painting on her face with light. It seemed that the more we did together, the more we wanted to do. It was never tiring for me to shoot her. It was never difficult. It was always a pleasure."

Carole Lombard, who bought most of her clothes with the still camera in mind, was a photographer's delight. She approached each sitting with almost as much care as a screen role. She would meet with the photographer perhaps a week before each session to discuss the type of photographs that would be taken, the backgrounds, and the wardrobe she should get for it. In her eight years at Paramount the studio released more than seventeen hundred portraits of her—and this does not include all the other types of stills and the portraits taken when she was on loan-out to other studios. Engstead, who adored Lombard and loved working with her, praised her contribution to the success of her portraits: "Carole always gave her complete cooperation. She loved good photographs—knew about lighting and how to pose—and had no inhibitions about being photographed, so it was possible to shoot her any way you wanted and she gave all the time it needed." Hurrell looked at his old photographs with amazement:

I was so energetic in those days, so full of my own impulses. I worked so fast— it was as if I were out of control. I don't know now how I did it. When I look at them and think about it, why, I would be up and down that ladder, focus, up and down again, and shoot the picture in maybe two or three seconds. I was always fighting myself to keep from being stereotyped. I was always trying to think, "Let's see, this time you gotta do it differently. Eliminate that top light, or just put cross-lights . . . keep things lively, keep them alive." I did enjoy shooting stars. That's why I kept working at it. I enjoyed them because they had that wonderful feeling about being photographed and made you pleased about working.

By 1936 Garbo had completed her major film roles; Dietrich, severed from von Sternberg, would never again be treated with such sublime attention and would have to survive simply as an actress and a singer. With time, everybody got wise. The stars soon learned (or thought they did) which side of their face photographed best and refused any other angle or destroyed any photographs taken accidentally. The style of photography that emerged and was labeled by the publicity department as "glamour" became by the end of the decade something done with lights that could be used to sell anything from cigarettes to dog food. The photographers whose reputations had been established by their studio work found that they could command larger fees working freelance. After 1939 the captions that normally had gone with the portraits that were sent out to the publications no longer included the name of the photographer. The effects of fine photography still lingered on, even as film got faster, lenses sharper, cameras more manageable, and negatives smaller; but by the beginning of the 1940's, much of the great work was over.

One of the most celebrated close-ups in the history of the American cinema is the lingering final shot of Greta Garbo in *Queen Christina*

(1933). Like a figurehead she stands at the bow of the ship that will carry her away from her homeland, alone. The lover for whom she abdicated the throne has been killed in a senseless duel. The old galleon plows through the waves, and the expression on her face as she gazes out and beyond, silent and immobile, is haunting. For years film historians debated what must have been going on in Garbo's mind to produce such a profoundly felt expression. Finally the director, Rouben Mamoulian, revealed his secret: "I told her to empty her mind of everything and to look without blinking, to make her face a blank parchment on which everybody who saw it could write what they felt. This was Garbo's achievement." What Mamoulian had done was to film Garbo posing exactly as she would for a still portrait. As the camera moves toward her, crossing the space that separates long shot from close-up, she looks straight ahead. The only movement is her hair and cloak being blown by a sea breeze. Her eyes—fathomless, unblinking—gaze steadily into the camera, which comes to rest a few feet before her in a tight close shot. Every aspect of Garbo's countenance is exposed to our scrutiny; every eyelash, every pore of her skin is there for us to consider.

Nothing moves on the screen.

Louise Brooks said, "When you think of it, what people remember of those stars is not from films, but *one* essential photograph: Dietrich—heavy-lidded, sucked-in cheeks / Keaton—sad little boy / Crawford—staring self-admiration / Gable—smiling, darling. And when I think of Garbo I do not see her moving in any particular film. I see her staring mysteriously into the camera. No matter how many times I've seen her in films, that is how I always see her. She is a still picture—unchangeable."

Greta Garbo. Photographed by Clarence S. Bull.

RUTH HARRIET LOUISE

Ruth Harriet Louise with starlet Joan Crawford, May 14, 1928

Her photographs were magnificent. I took orders from her as I would have from D. W. Griffith. —Lillian Gish

Ruth Harriet Louise Sandrich, who dropped her family name when she went into business, was a rabbi's daughter from New York. She studied photography before opening her own studio in New Brunswick, New Jersey. In 1925 she went to Los Angeles to visit her brother, Mark Sandrich, who became one of the most successful directors of 1930's musicals. Her cousin, the actress Carmel Myers (best known for her role as the temptress in the 1926 *Ben-Hur*), introduced Ruth to MGM's publicity director, Howard Strickling. Strickling was so impressed with her work that she was given her own portrait gallery at the age of nineteen. At that time, William Randolph Hearst had just moved his independent film distribution company, Cosmopolitan, from Paramount to MGM. Hearst was also very much impressed with Louise's work, and he wanted her to photograph his star, Marion Davies, which could account for the extraordinary terms of Louise's contract with the studio: she had approval of the photographs that were to be used; the studio agreed that all her photographs would bear her name; and Louis B. Mayer personally granted her the privilege of photographing people outside the studio. (When, five years later, on his own time and outside the studio grounds, George Hurrell took photographs of an actress not connected with the studio, it provoked a confrontation that ended with his resignation.)

Ruth Harriet Louise almost never shot a close-up.* Those delicate expressions that are the hallmark of her best work were not done in the camera but were the result of careful cropping. What the public finally saw in magazines had begun on the set, where Louise would watch her

---

* This observation is based on the author's interviews with Al St. Hilaire and a study of some of Louise's original negatives, none of which included any close-ups, but from which several of her famous close-up prints were made.

sitters at work. By the time they sat before her in the gallery, she knew what she wanted to capture and was able to translate their physicality—their energy—onto their faces.

Nina Mae McKinney—a lithe, vibrant, attractive girl from Harlem—was discovered by director King Vidor for his all-black musical, *Hallelujah!* (MGM, 1929). She sits, vulnerable and unsophisticated, in Louise's gallery on the third floor of the cutting department building, sporting a toque and wearing a sleazy little dress from the film, her arms bare—a shy creature, street wise and worldly, as radiant, as frightened, and as hopeful as Iphigenia, the child bride of death.

John Gilbert was the dashing, romantic idol of the 1920's. Louise conveys his sexuality and sensitivity and the intensity of his brooding nature. If we had never known the movies that made his name, if we had known only his pitiful downfall and had seen him only at the end of his career—a tired, prematurely aged shadow of his former self, playing the foil to Garbo's Queen Christina—Louise's portraits would rectify the conclusions we would have drawn. From the portrait we can understand what the remote Garbo once loved about this man, so that long after their affair had ended, she felt it necessary to oppose Louis B. Mayer and demand that Gilbert, almost forgotten, be given the coveted role instead of the younger, and potentially more suitable, Laurence Olivier.

Louise was trusted by the people she photographed. She was their age and was a fellow artist who shared their sensitivities and doubts. As a woman, alone in what was then an essentially male profession, she would have understood and sympathized with the young Greta Garbo, the foreigner, awkward with words in a language she hardly knew, cut off from her homeland, her sense of isolation and estrangement only increased by a meteoric rise to popularity she would be the last to understand, with few trustworthy friends to guide her through the swarm of admirers.

There was a rapport between them. In her photographs of Garbo, Louise gives us a living woman—warm, young, potentially approachable. At this time (1928, during the shooting of *Woman of Affairs*), three of the most distinguished photographers of the day—Edward Steichen, Nickolas Muray, and Arnold Genthe—each had a short session with Garbo, and all of their photographs, now so famous, were of the immutable, remote goddess, the woman no one would presume to call Greta.

By 1930 Garbo had become inviolate. Even under the most intense scrutiny, on screen or in still photographs, with the camera a breath away from her face, she could no longer be invaded. She had become an icon, an object to adore, but not to touch. She had become "Garbo."

Louise left MGM in the first months of 1930 to marry the director Leigh Jason. For a time she worked as a freelancer, photographing stars who were not under contract to a studio. She was hired briefly by Samuel Goldwyn to photograph his highly touted Russian star, Anna Sten. (Sten was to have been Goldwyn's Garbo.) Little of Louise's subsequent work has survived.

Mae Murray, 1926

Renée Adorée, in costume by Erté for La Boheme, *1926*

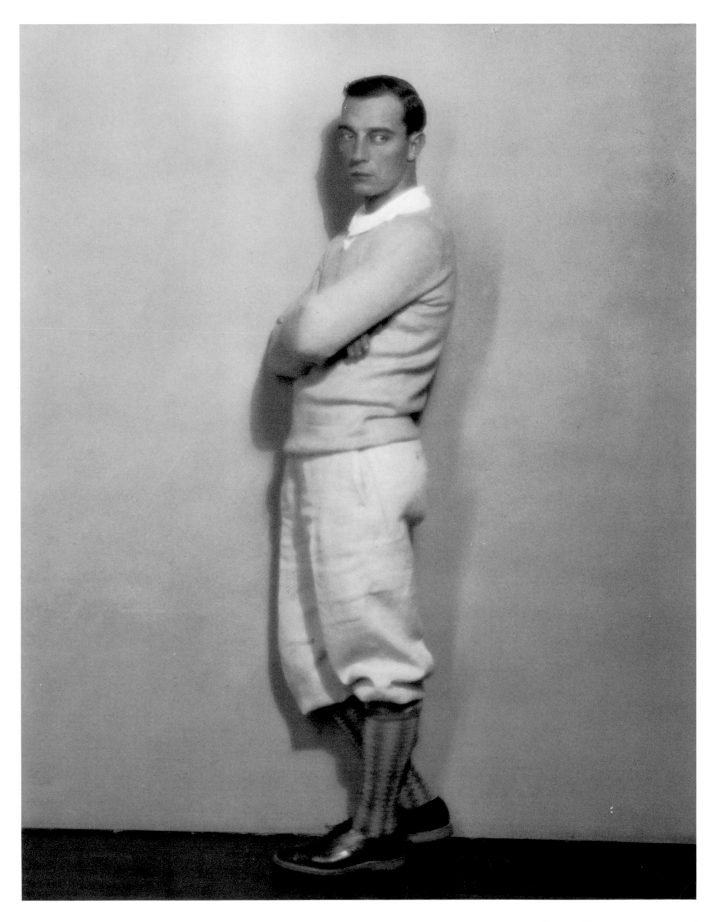

Buster Keaton, 1927 or 1928

Marion Davies, photographed for Lights of Old Broadway *(1925)*

Norma Shearer, 1929

John Gilbert, 1927

Nina Mae McKinney, 1929

Loretta Young, 1928

Greta Garbo, 1925

1927

1927

Greta Garbo in costume for The Temptress *(1926). Printed by Ted Allan in 1980.*

1927

ERNEST BACHRACH

*Ernest Bachrach photographing Dolores Del Rio and Gene Raymond
for* Flying Down to Rio *(1933)*

Ernest Bachrach was one of the most influential and admired of all the Hollywood portrait photographers. He headed the photographic department at RKO from its inception in 1929 until his retirement in the late 1950's. While there he controlled every aspect of the department, from publicity and advertising to hiring and training upcoming still and portrait photographers like Alex Kahle, Gaston Longet, and Robert Coburn as his assistants. He also shot and custom printed most of the portraits of the stars employed by RKO during these decades, among them the young Joel McCrea, Ann Harding, Dolores Del Rio, Irene Dunne, Fred Astaire, Gwili Andre, and Katharine Hepburn. Bachrach was also a frequent contributor to *American Cinematographer* and *International Photographer*.

For Gloria Swanson, who had been photographed by everybody, "there was no other photographer in the world," recalled Bob Coburn. She first met Bachrach after having left Hollywood for Paramount's Astoria studio in New York in 1923, and he became the still photographer on the films she made there. When Swanson formed her own company in 1926 and moved back to Hollywood, Bachrach went with her and shot the stills and the portraits for those films, among them *Sadie Thompson* and *Queen Kelly* (both 1928) and *The Trespasser* (1929).

"As a rule I have found it highly advantageous to know my sitters relatively well," Bachrach explained. "Like a director, I play upon his or her emotions and induce the mood and expressions that I desire."

Perhaps the most difficult subject of great photography is the person who is recognized and admired for his or her perfect beauty. There exist many photographs of classically beautiful women—such as Hedy Lamarr and Dolores Del Rio—whose flawless skin and perfectly balanced features left not only their generation but also their photographers speechless. The way to photograph them was to keep the face expressionless; animating the face distorted the perfection. Dolores Del Rio quickly became reduced to the clothes she wore and the sets she decorated, like any other extraordinary but inanimate object. Her career in America was restricted because of her kind of beauty. How rare, then, to find portraits like the ones Bachrach took of her in the years she worked at RKO. These photographs convey a near-mystical quality and reveal a glimpse into a quiet but decisive Latin temperament.

Bachrach: "Portraiture is very closely akin to cinematography. The cinematographer has very little need for accessories in the making of close-ups; all he needs is a face and some lights and shadows. And that is all the portrait artist needs. Occasionally—but only occasionally—minor props are useful."

The eccentric and vital Katharine Hepburn was a subject close to Bachrach's heart. Her dancer's body made her a wonderful model; her intelligence, enthusiasm, and flair made her face a source of inspiration for his camera. Hepburn, as serenely lovely as Del Rio, as gloriously handsome as Joel McCrea, and as enigmatic as Garbo, was still an American original:

These men, my God! These men were responsible for covering up a lot of faults in a lady's face. All the ladies were meant to be absolutely beautiful, and they sure weren't. Of course, photographically you would have to tick at a different rate than most people. You have to be like lightning, or so slow that they reach and try to catch you. There was a whole attitude that went with those old films. You can't imitate it. You had to believe it. Nobody has been able to re-create the Scott Fitzgerald stories. And I think I understand why—because of the madness of that era. . . . They're lethargic today compared to them; they were vital and frivolous and wicked and funny. And it was all done with wit. Today there is no wit.

Mae Murray, 1921

Evelyn Brent, 1931

Gloria Swanson, 1929

Mary Astor, 1931

Dolores Del Rio, 1932

1931

Fred Astaire, 1937

Gwili Andre, 1933

Carole Lombard, 1939

Katharine Hepburn, 1936

Katharine Hepburn, 1933

Katharine Hepburn, 1935

Katharine Hepburn, 1933

JOSEF VON STERNBERG

Eugene Robert Richee

Don English

William Walling, Jr.

Joseph von Sternberg, 1939. Photographed by Lazlo Willinger.

Josef von Sternberg was capable of everything that had to do with the making of a film—writing, designing, lighting, photographing, editing, scoring. Because of his meticulous attention to detail and his exacting eye, the merits of the cameramen, writers, actors, photographers, costume designers, and set designers who worked on his films resided not in their own originality but in their ability to satisfy von Sternberg. His genius was to inspire genius. The people who worked with him did work that was as good for others; but none did work that was better, and rarely did their work fit as sublimely into the whole as it did in von Sternberg's films.

The photographs here, all of Marlene Dietrich, were taken by three highly skilled photographers: Eugene Robert Richee, who ran Paramount's portrait gallery and shot most of Dietrich's portraits; Don English, one of the industry's top publicity and still photographers, who shot the stills on all of Dietrich's pictures for Paramount; and William Walling, Jr., who had been an actor, assistant director, assistant cameraman, and still photographer before joining Paramount in 1932 to head the second portrait gallery and who shot Dietrich on two separate occasions in 1934.

Marlene Dietrich being photographed by Eugene R. Richee in her home in Hollywood, 1935. John Engstead (at far right) arranged and posed her sittings after she and von Sternberg had stopped working together.

Eugene Robert Richee got his job at Paramount in the late teens through his friend Clarence S. Bull. He started shooting stills while Donald Biddle Keyes was taking portraits in the gallery. When Keyes left Paramount Richee took over, and for two decades he photographed the studio's stars, including Clara Bow, Gloria Swanson, Rudolph Valentino, Louise Brooks, Claudette Colbert, Gary Cooper, Fredric March, and the Marx Brothers. He was capable of re-creating the von Sternberg / Dietrich effect on the studio's other stars (see his photograph of Carole Lombard on page 33).

Richee was the perfect technician for von Sternberg, who controlled the sittings, supervised the lighting setups, and directed the action just as he did on the studio floor. When Dietrich's collaboration with von Sternberg ended, Richee continued to take her portraits, which retained the look of the von Sternberg originals.

After leaving Paramount in 1941 to be replaced by A. L. "Whitey" Schaefer, Richee worked at MGM doing portraits of Dietrich for *Kismet,* 1942, as well as other films and stars. In the late '40s, he worked at Warner Bros. where he took portraits of stars such as Ginger Rogers, Alexis Smith, Patricia Neal, and others.

Marlene Dietrich, photographed for Dishonored (*1931*)

1930

Photographed for Morocco (1930)

Photographed for Shanghai Express *(1932)*

Photographed for Morocco (*1930*)

Don English, 1934. Photographed by William Walling, Jr.

Don English's work fulfilled von Sternberg and Dietrich's demands, for besides taking the stills on the set of each of their films, he shot Dietrich in costume for the films' posters. In later years he went to work for the Walt Disney organization when they started to make live-action films, shooting both stills and portraits.

His photographs in this portfolio are part of a series taken of Dietrich aboard the train for *Shanghai Express* (1932).

Marlene Dietrich, photographed for Shanghai Express *(1932)*

William Walling, Jr., photographing Gail Patrick, 1939

Most of William Walling's subjects were Paramount's young actors and starlets (Ray Milland, Dorothy Lamour, Ann Sheridan), and the more difficult of the studio's older stars (W. C. Fields, Charles Laughton). Walling photographed Dietrich when Richee was on vacation and the studio was desperate for photographs of her in her new movie, *The Devil Is a Woman* (1935).

"With Dietrich a session would last the day," Walling explained. "When she came into the gallery, von Sternberg came with her. He dressed the set the way he wanted it. He wanted the camera high; he wanted it low; he would have somebody put it up or down, till it was exactly right. He talked to her in German. I don't know what the hell he was telling her. But Dietrich's ability to turn it on and off made photographing her very exciting."

Marlene Dietrich, 1934

Marlene Dietrich, 1934

GEORGE HURRELL

George Hurrell photographing MGM starlet Dorothy Jordan, 1931

George Hurrell left MGM in 1932, but he continued to photograph their top stars for the rest of the decade. Joan Crawford and Norma Shearer were adamant about having Hurrell shoot all their important glamour sittings in conjunction with every new film. He was one of the few Hollywood portrait photographers whose work appeared in the New York fashion magazines. For *Esquire* he did a series of glamour portraits that became as famous throughout the late thirties and the war years as Vargas pin-ups and pretty girls on army barracks walls. "I was always fighting myself to keep from being stereotyped, always trying to think, let's see, this time you gotta do it differently—eliminate that top light, or just put cross lights."

Hurrell photographed Joan Crawford for almost ten years. In their work together she was willing to give her all, for she knew Hurrell's pictures would enhance her image. In the photographs here she inhabits a sea of furs; her strength is revealed in the cut of her dress, the tilt of her head, the sweep or curl of her hair:

You can't just stand there saying, "Look this way, look that way, now smile." I had to do it fast by keeping up a certain action, yelling, hollering, moving things around, keeping up the pace. . . .

I lit men differently, with much more definite front light. . . . I would first get them to feel natural. Not slouching or falling apart—you had to remember that there were a million women out there waiting to see this picture, and he's got to look like "If I can just get my hands on that guy." So you had to give the photographs that "Why don't you come up and see me sometime?" look.

A lot of the things here were done with one spotlight—it gave a kind of dramatic look. It created dark shadows under the eyes and the nose. But you had to be careful so you didn't just get a photograph of a face hidden in the shadows. A lot of the things I did with Crawford and Harlow were shot that way—just a single light on the face, and everything else black.

I did enjoy shooting film stars. I enjoyed working with them because they had a wonderful feeling about being photographed.

Clark Gable, 1931

213

Myrna Loy, 1933

Clark Gable, 1933

Norma Shearer, 1932

Norma Shearer, 1932

Jean Harlow, 1935

Carole Lombard, 1938

Joan Crawford, 1935

Joan Crawford, 1932

Joan Crawford, 1932

1935

Joan Crawford, 1932

CLARENCE SINCLAIR BULL

Clarence Sinclair Bull photographing Clark Gable and Myrna Loy for Parnell (1937)

Clarence Sinclair Bull was born in Sun River, Montana, in 1896. In 1912 he went to the studio of the famous Western artist Charles Russell in the hope of becoming a painter, but Russell suggested that Bull might be better suited to photography. By the time he got to the University of Michigan, Bull had gained enough experience to allow him to photograph visiting celebrities for the local paper. In 1917 he went to Hollywood and got a job as an assistant cameraman at Metro Pictures. He would shoot stills of the stars during the production breaks, and in 1920 he was hired by Sam Goldwyn to do publicity stills of his studio stars. Goldwyn merged with Metro in 1924, and Bull was kept on as head of the Metro-Goldwyn-Mayer stills department.

Bull remained at MGM for the rest of his career. Though he was experienced in every branch of his department, from printing to retouching, his fame rests on his photographic collaboration with Greta Garbo. With one exception (Hurrell in 1930 for *Romance*; see page oo), Bull photographed Garbo from 1929, shortly before Ruth Harriet Louise left MGM, until 1941, when the actress retired from the screen.

These portraits of Garbo are from four sessions arranged to promote her newest films between August 1929 and December 1932. They usually lasted half a day each, depending on the costumes and hairstyles worn by her character in the film. Virgil Apger, Bull's assistant during this time, described the mood of these sessions: "Garbo would arrive quietly. We would be getting things ready and setting up lights, and maybe an hour would pass and we wouldn't realize she was there. She liked one sort of lighting, high-key and very little fill. Garbo didn't tell people what to do, but that's what she liked. One key light and one top light. We used a long 14-inch or 22-inch lens to get those close-ups. She didn't like the camera too close because she'd get too conscious of it. Sometimes Bull might suggest an idea. They were nicely tuned to each other."

Pointing to portraits of Garbo spread out before him, Bull said, "I never had to say 'hold it' or 'still, please.' All I did was light that face and wait, and watch. Her face was the most inspirational I ever photographed."

Hedy Lamarr, 1938

Gary Cooper, 1932

Greta Garbo, photographed for The Kiss *(1929)*

Photographed for The Kiss (1929)

Photographed for Inspiration *(1931)*

Photographed for Mata Hari (1932)

Photographed for Mata Hari (1932)

Photographed for As You Desire Me *(1932)*

Greta Garbo, 1932

LASZLO WILLINGER

Laszlo Willinger with Ava Gardner, 1943

When Laszlo Willinger arrived in Hollywood in July 1937 under contract to MGM, he had already been a photographer for the famous German magazine *Berliner Illustrierte* and had established himself in European film studios as one of the foremost photographers of film stars of the period, among them Marlene Dietrich, Emil Jannings, Isa Miranda, and Zarah Leander. Until his resignation from MGM in 1944, he was the studio's top photographer, shooting all of their stars and replacing George Hurrell as personal photographer to Norma Shearer and Joan Crawford. Although by the early 1940's Hollywood glamour photography was entering its decline, Willinger brought a freshness and energy to his portraits and gave his subjects a quality of intelligence. He described what it was like to work with the studio's leading stars:

A sitting with Shearer, that was like the King of England traveling. First there would be a great deal of diplomatic back and forth before I was even notified that she was available. I'd get a stage, set up fifteen to twenty sets, and light them, so that all she had to do was to move from one set to another. She had photos of the sets before she agreed. If that was okay, then you were finally told, "Thursday, 11 a.m., Miss Shearer." Thursday I'd be there with a makeup woman, a hairdresser, a man from Publicity to keep her busy and see that she turned up, two or three electricians, depending on the size of the set, a prop man, a grip, and a flower man . . . and my own two assistants. After three or four last-minute cancellations (that's the way she operated—that's the way all stars operated), she would show up. Then she worked. And she would work hard. Once you had her you tried to take as many pictures as you could, because you knew you wouldn't have her for another six months. A good session with her or Crawford would be two to three hours. By that time everybody was pretty tired. Changing clothes, which had to be done between each setup, is tiring.

Crawford was a woman who worked with the photographer rather than saying, "Show me what you can do." She would suggest things. She was a harder worker than anybody I knew. She loved being photographed. And that shows.

Glamour was one of the few English words I'd never heard before I went to America. I remember once talking to Howard Strickling, and he said, "I want lots of glamour," and I said, "What's glamour?" And he said, "You know, a sort of suffering look." So there wasn't much laughing in those photos. You couldn't have happy sex. Sex and earnestness—together those spelled glamour.

When I started out in Germany in the late 1920's, photographers used either daylight or a very diffused light. I never did. I used spots—arcs, which give you a point source of light.

Dietrich lent herself to the dramatic lighting von Sternberg set up for her, and so did Crawford, because her eyes were very large. But you couldn't have used that von Sternberg lighting on Shearer—her eyes wouldn't have shown at all. When Hedy Lamarr made her first film at MGM, they were specifically trying to make her into a new Dietrich, and they photographed her using the Dietrich lighting setup. But it didn't quite work. For one thing, her face was a little rounder. So this light doesn't quite work for everybody—you need a specific kind of face for it.

Norma Shearer, photographed for Marie Antoinette *(1937)*

Ingrid Bergman, 1940

Hedy Lamarr, 1939

Clark Gable, 1938

Myrna Loy, 1937

Joan Crawford, 1939

Tyrone Power, 1938

Joan Crawford and Clark Gable, photographed for Strange Cargo *(1940)*

Vivien Leigh, photographed for Waterloo Bridge *(1940)*

Marlene Dietrich, 1942

275

Notes on Other Photographers

Sources

Index

Notes on Other Photographers

VIRGIL APGER

When Virgil Apger retired from his job as Metro-Goldwyn-Mayer's gallery portrait photographer in 1969, he had been there forty years. For twenty of those years he was the only gallery photographer on the lot.

Apger's interest in photography began when he was a child in Goodland, Idaho. His father, the local sheriff, took photographs of the town's criminals. Virgil worked as an usher and assistant to the projectionist of the town's only movie theatre. His first job in films was as a transportation man and laborer for the Mack Sennett Studios. In 1929 his brother-in-law, Eugene R. Richee, who was head of the portrait gallery at Paramount, hired Apger as his assistant. Apger developed Richee's negatives, worked with the dryers, and made prints. He recalled: "Gene never left a sitting with fewer than a hundred negatives, which had to be retouched and printed."

In 1930 Apger moved to MGM as Clarence S. Bull's assistant. He described what it was like to work for Bull:

When Bull worked with Garbo, I was the guy changing lights and generally assisting Clarence. Garbo liked to take things easy. She was a natural model. All Clarence had to do was to set the lights and squeeze the bulb. Hurrell's method wouldn't have worked with Garbo—she didn't like any fussing. There would just be the three of us on her sittings—Clarence, me, and the electrician. Bull would suggest ideas to her, but mostly she would bring the expressions that she had from the movie.

When Jean Harlow gave Apger his start as a production still photographer by requesting him for *China Seas* (1935), he had already worked for the publicity department. From then on he shot the stills on all her films. "Doing stills was invaluable training for gallery work," Apger explained.

Apger's enthusiasm on the set made him extremely popular with the stars, and Greer Garson, whose films he worked on, requested him for her portrait photographer. It was the stills he had taken on *Mrs. Miniver* (1942) that won him the only Academy Award ever given for Best Production Still.

In 1947 Apger was put in charge of the portrait gallery at MGM, and for the next twenty years he shot all of their stars: Esther Williams, Clark Gable, Lana Turner, Greer Garson, Judy Garland, Robert Taylor, Joan Crawford, Barbara Stanwyck, Kay Kendall, Stewart Granger, Ava Gardner, Grace Kelly, Elizabeth Taylor. Between 1948 and 1952, Apger had the distinction of having more magazine covers—among them, *Life, Look,* and *Photoplay*—than all of the other photographers at all of the other studios combined.

Apger's work—stylish, glamorous, imaginative—stood apart even in the lackluster fifties. Here are some of his reflections on his profession and on the stars he worked with:

Once you got her into the gallery, Esther Williams loved being photographed and fell into a pose with great ease. Hedy Lamarr couldn't. She thought she knew it all and was forever telling you what to do. She was beautiful—she had great skin texture—but I don't recall anybody saying they enjoyed shooting her. She never came alive, except to keep making damned uncouth remarks to the people I had around me.

Now Joan Crawford was a swell person to work with. So was Ava [Gardner]. She was open to ideas, ready for anything. She wasn't just beautiful. She knew that we had a lot of people to please, and she would cooperate all the way. People like that keep you fresh in your work.

ERIC CARPENTER

Eric Carpenter began working as a plasterer during the Depression. In 1933 he joined Metro-Goldwyn-Mayer as an office boy. He succeeded Virgil Apger as Clarence S. Bull's assistant and continued in that capacity until he got his union card,

. . . on the condition that I work in the gallery and not as a still or publicity photographer, because that area was all sewn up. I didn't have my own gallery, so I set one up on the set and shot there. That was at the end of 1939. . . . My first solo assignment—and this was a case of make or break—was to photograph Norma Shearer. Willinger had been doing her portraits up until then, but I had heard that he wasn't happy just being her photographer, and she wanted someone loyal to her, so she was trying out new photographers. If she approved, I was in. Lucky for me she did. We did an outside session down by her beach house. . . . I had already learned a lot by watching Hurrell and Bull, but my "style" was trial and error.

With his spirited and beautiful portraits, Carpenter quickly became the favorite photographer of the studio's rising young stars, like Ava Gardner, Mickey Rooney, James Craig, Esther Williams, Judy Garland, and Lana Turner. His rapport with Turner began when she signed with MGM and lasted up to her departure from the studio in the late fifties. Carpenter was responsible for most of her torrid, memorable gallery portrait sittings. His photographs of her are lush and immediate in dazzling whites and sophisticated, plungingly deep blacks. More dynamic than almost any of the other glamour portraits of the era, their effect recalled the Harlow portraits and anticipated the ones of Monroe at Fox in the early fifties—acres of white fur, opalescent skin, poses inviting by their ease.

Carpenter once explained:

The only secret of good work is to get the star to have confidence in you so that you can try to do something interesting. Stars appreciated what you were trying to do. The publicity department kept asking for glorified passport photos, which was what the newspapers could use. It was always a fight to get some shading into those pictures.

After the war Carpenter left the profession to join his brother in the shipyard business, but by 1950 he was back at MGM, this time as a production still photographer—a job he held until his retirement in the sixties—working on films like *Quentin Durward* (1955), *Beau Brummel* (1954), and *Mutiny on the Bounty* (1962).

JACK FREULICH

Jack Freulich had emigrated from Europe with his family, including brother Roman, a still photographer at Universal until he left in 1945 to head the portrait gallery at Republic Pictures. Jack Freulich photographed all of Universal's silent-screen stars, including Mary Philbin, Priscilla Dean, Erich von Stroheim, and Laura La Plante, and early sound stars like Bette Davis. (His photographs of her belied the studio's reason for canceling her contract: they said she had as much sex appeal as comedian Slim Summerville.)

Freulich committed suicide in 1936, shortly after being replaced as head of the gallery at Universal by his former still man, Ray Jones. Ed Estabrook, who knew Freulich well, said that when the aging Carl Laemmle sold his interest in the studio in 1935, the new broom sweeping through the organization cleared out many of the European Jewish émigrés related to Laemmle or to others on the staff, replacing them with gentiles.

ELMER FRYER

Elmer Fryer began working as a photographer in 1924. When Warner Bros. and First National Studios joined operations in 1929, Fryer replaced Fred Archer as head of the new Warner–First National stills department. During the 1930's he took portraits of Dolores Del Rio, Kay Francis, Barbara Stanwyck, Bette Davis, James Cagney, Errol Flynn, George Brent, and other Warner Bros. stars.

BUD GRAYBILL

Bud Graybill—a native of Los Angeles—had his first contact with the film world in 1922 with a paper route near the MGM (then Triangle) studio, selling papers to stars, among them Mae Murray and Robert Z. Leonard. "I grew up at MGM," he explained. "Every summer from 1924 on I'd work in a different department. I worked as an extra, as a trick man, in the special effects department, in production, and in casting. I would make enough money scraping wax in the sound department to go to school all year."

Graybill's interest in photography began at UCLA. While studying business administration he started taking pictures for the school yearbook. When he graduated in 1933, MGM publicity head Howard Strickling hired him as a publicity assistant. After three years of writing handouts and campaign books, his intimate knowledge of the needs of the publicity department enabled him at last to join the photographer's union.

My first assignment was a circus picture, called O'Shaughnessy's Boy [1935]. Can you imagine shooting action with an 8 × 10 camera? From then on it was one picture after another, until finally I got the publicity assignment, which was wonderful. I'd go on every set each morning and shoot publicity stills for pictures like A Tale of Two Cities [1935], Romeo and Juliet [1936], and *Captains Courageous* [1937]. This led to my doing layouts on assignment from the gallery, working on the set or in the stars' homes, catching them in informal poses (or what we called posed informality) that were designed to be spreads in the rotogravure sections of the newspapers around the country. There was a team of us specializing in this sort of work—Virgil Apger, Eric Carpenter, Frank Tanner, and others.

Graybill became so adept at pleasing the stars that they frequently asked him to photograph their parties, christenings, and other private affairs.

Some days I'd be shooting fashion for Maureen O'Sullivan; then I'd be doing glamour for Lana Turner; the next day I'd be on the set doing publicity, taking pictures that would make good layouts. And when political or military statesmen visited and the whole studio would turn out to greet them on a sound stage, I'd cover it, too. To me the thirties were the optimum years of the entire business.

RAY JONES

Ray Jones began taking stills at Universal in 1922 (Jack Freulich was head of the newly formed stills department), and he spent most of his career there, although he left from time to work for other companies. Jones shot stills and portraits for the Sennett Studios but returned to Universal in 1930 as Freulich's assistant. During this period he photographed such stars as Irene Dunne, John Boles, Jean Harlow, Boris Karloff, and Tala Birell, then being heavily promoted by the studio as their threat to Garbo and Dietrich.

In 1933 the cameramen's union called its people out in sympathy with the sound men, who were striking for recognition of their union, and many photographers moved to better-paying jobs at other studios. Ray Jones joined Fox to head their stills department, while Otto Dyar, formerly portrait photographer at Paramount, took over their portrait gallery. During the year that Dyar spent in London in 1934 shooting portraits of Gaumont's stars to help promote them to the American public, Jones took over the Fox portrait gallery and photographed Lilian Harvey, Janet Gaynor, the Harlowesque Alice Faye, Lew Ayres, Will Rogers, and others. Jones left Fox in 1934 to work as a freelancer, during which time he shot stills on two of DeMille's films, *Cleopatra* (1934) and *The Crusades* (1935), but he rejoined Universal the following year to take over Freulich's job.

In the next two decades at Universal, Jones was responsible for most of the portraits of the studio's top stars under contract, including Danielle Darrieux, Marlene Dietrich, and Maria Montez, and he shot most of the extant photographs of Deanna Durbin. Jones taught photography and wrote about it during his years at the studio and after his retirement in the fifties.

DONALD BIDDLE KEYES

Donald Biddle Keyes, a pioneer photographer and motion-picture cameraman, started, out as a publicity photographer at the Ince Triangle studios at Culver City (later MGM). After World War I he moved to the Lasky studios, photographing such stars as Rudolph Valentino, Pola Negri, Gloria Swanson, and Wallace Reid, and taking stills on a number of their films. He left the studio in 1922 and alternated between working as first cameraman and still photographer. The photographs he took of Ann Sheridan to promote *Winter Carnival* (United Artists, 1939) appeared on the covers of seven national magazines, including *Life,* which also ran a story on Sheridan. From 1945 until his retirement in 1954, Keyes was a contract photographer for Republic Pictures.

MADISON LACY

Madison Lacy began taking photographs as a child in 1907. He started working in a motion-picture lab and got into the stills department at the Griffith studio through Billy Bitzer, Griffith's cameraman.

In 1919 Lacy joined Hal Roach's company, where, as he put it, "I had about nine occupations besides taking stills." In 1924 he went independent, working on Westerns "and on the early 'states' rights' pictures, which were really terrible. Real quickies. You couldn't do much of anything creative there. You couldn't do much of anything except shoot!"

For a time Lacy worked at Paramount, where he shot the stills on Erich von Stroheim's celebrated *The Wedding March* (1928). "Stroheim shot scenes in a brothel that could never have been shown on the screen, and I shot the stills," he explained.

In 1933, Lacy went to work at Warner Bros. Throughout the thirties and into the forties he shot stills on many of their films, besides doing publicity and specializing in "leg art"—those widely circulated Busby Berkeley "cuties." "Some of those girls, like Toby Wing, were used more for stills than for anything else," Lacy explained. "It was difficult to make them look very different, because Busby Berkeley personally selected them, and they all looked alike!" Lacy also photographed Harlow look-alike Mary Dees, so catching the resemblance that she was hired to replace the deceased star in the uncompleted scenes of Harlow's last picture, *Saratoga* (1937).

Lacy was proudest of his years with David O. Selznick, whom he joined after leaving the armed services, where he had worked in the photographic section. He shot many of the stills and special portrait work for *Spellbound* (1945) and *Duel in the Sun* (1947). "Selznick was a great publicist. Everybody working for him was proud to be having something to do with him."

During Lacy's fifty years as a photographer, he shot the most famous beauties to come out of Hollywood, some of whose potential first emerged in his portraits, such as the nubile seventeen-year-old Lana Turner. Lacy: "I think probably everything to do with glamour—real glamour photography as we know it—originated with Hollywood."

BERT LONGWORTH

Between 1928 and 1939, Bert "Buddy" Longworth took the bulk of the celebrated stills for the production numbers of the kaleidoscopic Warner Bros. musicals (*Forty-second Street,* 1933; *Gold Diggers of 1933;* etc.). He had started out in 1910 with his own portrait gallery in Detroit and had established the first postcard photo service in America before becoming a news photographer for the Chicago *Tribune.* Longworth joined Universal Pictures in 1921, where he shot stills for *The Hunchback of Notre Dame* (1923) and *The Phantom of the Opera* (1925), among other films.

At MGM Longworth shot stills for Garbo's first films. These pictures —including Garbo and Gilbert locked in embrace from *Flesh and the Devil* (1926)—are some of the most instantly recognizable images from silent films and became the most frequently reproduced stills of that era. In 1937 Longworth published a private edition of his photographs entitled *Hold Still Hollywood.*

AL ST. HILAIRE

Al St. Hilaire began his career in photography in 1930, working for Ruth Harriet Louise during the last months of her term at MGM, washing and drying her prints and delivering them to the publicity department. "When I joined MGM I got a job in the script department at twelve dollars a week," he said. "I wasn't especially interested in photography, but at seventeen dollars a week the money was better." When George Hurrell was brought in to take over her studio, St. Hilaire became his assistant. "It was watching George work that made me want to become a photographer," he explained. In 1938 St. Hilaire branched out to become a still photographer, working at Columbia in the forties. In the sixties he photographed productions like *Judgment at Nuremburg* (1961) and *It's a Mad, Mad, Mad, Mad World* (1963).

SCOTTY WELBOURNE

Scotty Welbourne replaced Elmer Fryer at Warner Bros. in 1941, photographing many of the studio's newer stars, including Lana Turner, Ann Sheridan, Ida Lupino, Humphrey Bogart, and Alexis Smith, as well as Marlene Dietrich and Merle Oberon. (During the shooting of *Fools for Scandal* (1938), he took 686 pictures of Carole Lombard in one day.) Welbourne believed that the proper use of light and shadow was the answer to most of the photographer's problems and that "the photograph or the photographer must never overshadow the subject in importance [but] must always be of secondary importance to the star."

Welbourne left Warner Bros. in 1945 to set up, with Madison Lacy and former MGM publicity photographer Bud Graybill, the stills department at Enterprise Productions, a short-lived production company that made three or four films, among them *Arch of Triumph* (1948).

Sources

Most of the quotations in this book are from interviews conducted between 1974 and 1979 by the author—in person, by telephone, and by letter—with the following photographers and stars: Ted Allan, Virgil Apger, Louise Brooks, Eric Carpenter, Robert W. Coburn, Bud Graybill, Katharine Hepburn, George Hurrell, Tom Jones, Madison Lacy, Rouben Mamoulian, Frank Powolny, Al St. Hilaire, Karl Struss, Loretta Young, William Walling, Jr., and Laszlo Willinger.

Other sources used were back issues of *American Cinematographer* and *International Photographer*, the magazine of the cameraman and photographer's union, which began publication in February 1929 and has proved to be one of the few reliable sources available for research on the early careers and opinions of the Hollywood still and portrait photographers. Especially useful were the following: Ernest Bachrach's "Personality and Pictorialism in Portraiture" (*American Cinematographer*, September 1932) and an article in *International Photographer* (February 1940); Clarence S. Bull's "The Stills Move the Movies" (*American Cinematographer*, November 1927) and an article in *International Photographer* (February 1940); Fred Hendrickson's biography in *International Photographer* (June 1940); Ira Hoke's "Some Historical Facts" (*International Photographer*, March 1941); Ray Jones's "Jones' People" (*International Photographer*, May 1938); Don MacKenzies's "The Life of a Stillman" (*International Photographer*, February 1934); and Scotty Welbourne's "Studio Portraits" (*International Photographer*, March 1941).

Also referred to and quoted from were the following books: John Drinkwater's *The Life and Adventures of Carl Laemmle* (London: Heinemann, 1931); John Engstead's *Star Shots* (New York: E.P. Dutton, 1978); Lillian Gish's *The Movies, Mr. Griffith and Me* (Englewood Cliffs, N.J.: Prentice-Hall, 1969); and Harry Reichenbach's (as told to David Freedman) *Phantom Fame: The Anatomy of Ballyhoo* (London: Noel Douglas, 1932).

Index

The text of this book is set on the Linotype in Fairfield, the first typeface from the hand of the distinguished American artist and engraver Rudolph Ruzicka. In its structure Fairfield displays the sober and sane qualities of a master craftsman whose talent has long been dedicated to clarity. It is this trait that accounts for for the trim grace and virility, the spirited design and sensitive balance of this original typeface.

Rudolph Ruzicka was born in Bohemia in 1883 and came to America in 1894. He set up his own shop devoted to wood engraving and printing in New York in 1913, after a varied career as a wood engraver, in photoengraving and bank-note printing plants, and as art director and free-lance artist. He designed and illustrated many books and created a considerable list of individual prints—wood engravings, line engravings on copper, aquatints. W. A. Dwiggins once wrote: "Until you see the things themselves you have no sense of the artist behind them. His outstanding quality, as artist and person, is *sanity*. Complete esthetic equipment, all managed by good sound judgment about ways and means, aims and purposes, utilities and 'functions'—and all this level-headed balance-mechanism added to the lively mental state that makes an artist an artist. Fortunate equipment in a disordered world. . . ." Ruzicka died in 1978.